Facing Every Mom's Fears

Other Books in This Series

HEARTS AT HOME® WORKSHOP SERIES

Facing Every Mom's Fears

A SURVIVAL GUIDE TO BALANCING FEAR WITH COURAGE

WITH LEADER'S GUIDE AND PERSONAL REFLECTIONS

Allie Pleiter

GRAND RAPIDS, MICHIGAN 49530 USA

We want to hear from you. Please send your comments about this book to us in care of zreview@zondervan.com. Thank you.

ZONDERVAN™

Facing Every Mom's Fears
Copyright © 2004 by Alyse Stanko Pleiter

Requests for information should be addressed to:

Zondervan, *Grand Rapids, Michigan 49530*

Library of Congress Cataloging-in-Publication Data

Pleiter, Allie, 1962–
    Facing every mom's fears: a survival guide to balancing fear with courage / Allie Pleiter.–1st ed.
        p. cm.–(Hearts at home workshop series)
    Includes bibliographical references.
    ISBN 0-310-25305-5
    1. Motherhood—Religious aspects—Christianity.   2. Fear—Religious aspects—Christianity.   I. Title.   II. Series.
    BV4529.18.P52 2004
    248.8'431—dc22
                                                                    2003025494

Published in association with Yates & Yates, LLP, Attorneys and Counselors, Suite 1000, Literary Agent, Orange, CA.

Interior design by Michelle Espinoza

Printed in the United States of America

04 05 06 07 08 09 10 /❖ DC/ 10 9 8 7 6 5 4 3 2 1

To the Next Generation of my little world:

Mandy, C.J., Savannah, Kaleah, Nora
And a new niece we will only just meet
by the time this book is printed.

May they all know courage, victory,
and God's boundlessly tender mercies.

CONTENTS

FOREWORD

My first child, Kristen, made her big-screen debut on March 28, 1988. Her daddy and I intently gazed at a grainy ultrasound picture projecting on a portable screen next to my side. As the comforting whooshing sounds of her sixteen-week-old prenatal heart filled the sterile office space, I sat there transfixed at the sight before my eyes.

This was my baby—right there on the screen before me. Unbelievable as it seemed, curled up safely just beneath the jellied surface of my ever-expanding belly was my daughter. Moment by moment my eyes tracked the technician's notations measuring the baby from crown to rump, across the skull, along the thighbone, and around the abdomen. Then my gaze rested on the image of her tiny head and neck area, and fear replaced any and all touchy-feely emotions I had up to that moment. With my eyes squinting tightly together, I leaned closer toward the shadowy image on the screen, drew in a panicked breath, and anxiously inquired, "Is her head attached to a neck? It doesn't look like my baby has a neck!"

God bless that technician whose name I have long forgotten. With blessed patience and first-time mother protocol, she carefully slid the transducer across my abdomen until she had a perfect image of Kristen. Indeed! There was a neck holding her beautiful head in place. Whew! One fear down . . . multiple more to go!

Nothing ratchets up the fear factor reality like the task of mothering. Whether we carry our babies physically in our wombs or count them "flesh of our flesh" through the transforming miracle of adoption, mothers all long to hear this reassuring truth: "Don't be afraid; everything is going to be all right."

Reading through Kristen's *When You Were Young* one-year memory book, I came across these journal entries:

- December 20, 1988: Pan Am Flight 103 crashed in Lockerbie, Scotland. Over two hundred people died, and so many were young college students. Oh, their poor mothers and fathers. It's so scary! I pray I never lose you. You are everything to me.
- January 7, 1989: First major hurt! A plaque hanging on the wall above your Johnny-Jump-Up fell and hit you right below your right eye. It gave you a black eye, and I think I cried harder and longer than you did. Good grief, how bad is it when it's your mom's poor judgment that causes you pain?
- February 4, 1989: We had our first night of sickness. You threw up about five times and scared Momma a lot! Daddy and I stayed up with you and nursed you through it. I love you so much, sweet girl. What would I do without you?
- February 14, 1989: Daddy was in a horrible car crash today. He had a compound fracture of his leg, crushed his right foot, had two thirds of his kneecap removed, and was bruised and cut up badly. I was terrified when the hospital called. I thought we were going to lose your daddy. How would I ever raise you without him? The fear of losing him had never crossed my mind ... until today.

On and on the entries went. More airline crashes, viruses that stumped medical experts, rumors of war, a 1989 Alar apple poisoning scare, and childhood spills and chills. Honestly, it was enough to make this self-professed "the glass is always half full" Momma want to build a shelter and go hide for a few years—or decades.

What I needed those many years ago (and still do, for I am the mother of two boys as well), and what you are holding in your hands right now, is just what we all need—a thought-ful, well-written book by a mother who has "been there, done that" in this arena of motherhood. As a woman who is still deep in the trenches of learning to trust God with her chil-dren, letting go of fear, and taming her panic-inducing imag-ination, I appreciate how Allie Pleiter's words speak to the fearmonger in each of us. Her words find us right where we are and reassure us that we do not have to live the rest of our mothering days tied up in knots of anxiety, worry, and para-lyzing fear.

So take the bubble-wrap off Junior, expel the "What next?" breath that you've been holding for the past few months (or years!), dare to free the baby from the confines of the playpen, and prepare to have your fearful Momma heart changed by the wit, wisdom, and writing of Allie Pleiter.

Julie Ann Barnhill

MY THANKS TO THE FOLKS WHO RIGGED MY WIRES

Many books are the product of far more than a single author. This book felt entirely too important to set on a single pair of shoulders, and so it required a great number of people to bring it to life. I'm indebted to many, many people who have helped me on this journey.

First, I must thank my family. They, more than anyone else, have endured my continual state of discomfort in writing this book. Writers are generally a tough lot to live with, but I've excelled at "high maintenance" during this project. Thank you, Mandy and CJ, for enduring a spectacularly grumpy mother. Your choruses of "You can do it, Mom!" are one of the most treasured by-products of this effort.

My gratitude goes out especially to my husband, Jeff, for enduring the whining, pondering, dreaded late-night questions, tantrums, and stacks of papers that seemed to take over our house on a regular basis. Most especially, dear, I am thankful for your understanding of the inexplicable but divine calling to write this book and your support under the strain.

If I wasn't whining to my family, I was whining to my friends. Thanks to all the "Sams" of my life, whacking me back from the edge or coming alongside me into the dark places. Christina, Martha, Charlene, Becky, Leeza, Kathy, Kathleen, the W.I.N.G.S. women, and so many more—you are God's hands, feet, and ears to me, and I am grateful.

Thanks as well to the women of Hearts at Home who are my cheering section there: Mary, Jill, Tonya, Jan, and so many others.

Only God could hook me up with earth's most famous wire-walking family—only to discover that many of them are in the family of faith. As such, Tony Hernandez and Lijana Wallenda Hernandez from the Actors Gymnasium were answers to prayer as the best high-wire teachers an adventurous housewife could want. Their insights, stories, and guidance made the process of learning fun and fantastic.

I owe much to my panel of experts: Dr. Todd Cartmell, Psy. D.; Dr. E. Maurlea Babb, LMFT, LPHA; Dr. Paulette Toburen, Psy. D.; and therapist Jenny Gresko, M.A., M.Div., L.C.P.C. Each of them generously shared their clinical and practical knowledge with me on a host of subjects, suggested books, gave me stories for examples, and encouraged me about the real need for this book.

I am grateful for the support I received from the folks at Zondervan. What a pleasure it is to do business—and the business of heaven—among friends.

Karen Solem, my agent, is no less than a godsend on a regular basis.

Most of all, though, I owe my thanks to the hundreds of women who trusted me with their deepest fears. This book is as much theirs as it is mine, and I am blessed and honored to share it with you.

With deepest thanks,
Allie

Chapter 1

THE HIGH-WIRE WALK
OF PARENTING

"I fear my child will choke if I don't watch her eat."

*"I'm afraid I'm smothering them in my worry that they
won't turn out right."*

"I fear my boys will marry women I can't stand."

*"I'm afraid to let my kids go to school. There is so much evil
out there—I just want to protect them from it all."*

High above the Center Ring

Like every parent on earth, I had no idea what I was getting into. If any of us knew what really lay ahead of us as mothers, I doubt we could muster the courage to go forward. If we had truth in advertising for babies, if the FDA required a list of parenting's potential side effects, we'd run for the hills. I believe that's why God makes babies so adorable—so cuddly and lovable and instantly attractive— it's the world's ultimate silver lining program. The good stuff of parenting has to be so very good because the bad stuff is so very bad.

Fear is the bad stuff of motherhood. Bringing a child into our lives is signing on for a multidecade program of worry, second-guessing, regret, and fear. I have two children, Amanda (Mandy) and Christopher (CJ), who have brought more joy, more love, and more worry into my life than I ever thought possible. I've been a parent for a dozen years now, as Mandy will turn twelve the month this book hits the shelves and CJ will turn eight shortly after. Things I thought I'd get used to, I never have. Things I thought would surely slay me have become ordinary, everyday parts of my life. *None* of it has gone the way I expected—in the very best and the very worst sense. I am a changed woman because I am a mother.

I am a changed woman because of this book as well. I wanted to write a book about fear because I believe it has such an enormous impact on how we parent. Few other factors control our actions, our thoughts, our abilities, and our limitations more deeply than fear.

Contemporary living gives women much to fear. True or not, parenting feels as though it has become more difficult than it has ever been. National events and the natural events of my own family have brought fears to light I would not have dreamed I owned.

It matters tremendously how we deal—or don't deal—with our fears. I hope you discover this book to be a useful companion on your journey to courage. Each chapter will focus on a dif-

> *Few other factors control our actions, our thoughts, our abilities, and our limitations more deeply than fear.*

ferent aspect of your fears as a woman and as a mother. You'll hear stories from my own life and from scores of women around me who shared their own experiences. Each chapter will offer you questions to help you face your fears, practical tips to fight your fears, and verses from the Bible to help find your faith in the face of fear.

If you learn nothing else from these pages, gain nothing from the practical tips, funny stories, useful insights, or psychological research, I hope you learn that *you are not the only woman to fear.* When I began soliciting feedback from women on the subject of fear, I recorded on cards what they told me. I gathered cards upon cards upon cards, building an enormous pile of responses from women across the country—women just like you. The quotes you see at the beginning of each section are the real words of mothers throughout the country who shared their fears with me— and now with you.

The universality of fear is astounding. I thought I knew what was coming, but I was wrong. I was unprepared for the startling expanse of pain, guilt, and worry as hundreds upon hundreds of women poured their souls out to me.

I wish you could see these precious cards that represent so many fears spread out on my dining room table. I pick up the card from over here, from the woman who is so certain she is failing her children and is sure she is the only woman on the planet feeling so scared and inept. I move her card over where there is a stack—astoundingly high—of women who have expressed the exact same emotion. I want to introduce these women to each other, to let them know they are not alone. And I want to let you know you are not alone.

> I want to introduce these women to each other, to let them know they are not alone. And I want to let you know you are not alone.

Come along with me on what has proven to be the most amazing journey of a lifetime. We'll draw courage from each other, from professionals who lent their expertise, from Scripture, and from the most unlikely metaphor you could imagine: a high wire.

Courageous parenting, I have discovered, is a high-wire act. A circus-worthy feat of daring. An act that seems too scary, too risky to be possible for mere mortals like us.

But it is possible for a host of reasons. Want to find out why?

Pass the popcorn, turn the pages, and let me show you.

Challenge 1:
We Find Fears We Never Knew We Had
If Only Chocolate Were Courage

My first instinct was to title this book *Fight Fear with Chocolate*. Not only did I figure this guaranteed me a run-away bestseller, but it would allow me and other chocoholic women around the globe justification for one of our favorite coping mechanisms. Silly as the chocolate title sounds, it's not too far off, is it? Making a beeline for the chocolate is a legendary tactic when fear or worry strikes a woman.

Now, we're no fools. We don't need anyone to tell us compensating with chocolate is not a good impulse. We know that already. Where fear is concerned, though, lots of our first impulses are unhealthy.

Daily life as a parent hands us many reasons to fear. When we are afraid, our responses range from the survival/instinctual based, to the wise and methodical, to the silly and reactionary. All are real. All are human. Not all are productive. Chocolate makes an especially fine example because it reminds us that while all fears feel real, not all responses get results.

Take the "Stomp and Hiss" for example. You know what I mean: that quick hiss of sucking my breath in through my teeth while I stomp my foot down on the brake and my hand flies out across a body—any body—blocking and protecting in an automotive near miss. I've done it a hundred times. I even do it during crises on television or in the movies.

I'm also the queen of holding my breath on the playground—so convinced my little one will fall to his imminent demise from the monkey bars. Now really, will sucking in my breath increase my son's safety? No, but I can't help doing it anyway. When my son is old enough to head for the skate park, I think I'm going to need medication.

You don't automatically pair up moms and fear. That is, until you're a parent yourself. With the exception of the occasional B movie or daytime drama, moms aren't associated with scary things. To the world we're "Mommy." The bastions of comfort. Warm cookies. Oatmeal. After-bath cuddles. Home. Moms are the spokeswomen for "It'll be all right."

> You don't automatically pair up moms and fear. That is, until you're a parent yourself.

It's what mothers are supposed to say, right? We're comforting creatures, the living symbols of unconditional love. We're the ones who are supposed to be there for you when no one else will even give you the time of day.

Those stereotypes didn't materialize out of thin air. In many ways, moms *are* all that. Parental love—especially a mother's love—is one of the most powerful forces on earth. Mother Nature. Mother tongue. The Mother of all _____ (insert any noun here). Our language is filled with references to the power of motherhood. While there are days when I'd pay any price for the first words out of my children's mouths in a crisis to be "Daaadddy!" you and I both know they are usually "Mooommm!" Even when Daddy is standing right next to them. That's because I am the mommy, and it is in the natural order of the universe that I am supposed to make it all better.

Moms protect. Even in the animal kingdom—what's the most dangerous animal? A mother protecting her young. You don't need to turn on Animal Planet to look for evidence of this; humankind is brimming with it. Want to watch a mild-mannered parent turn fierce? Threaten her child. The urge to protect our children wells up in us like the Cowardly Lion's new medal, and we roar. Even those of us who consider ourselves mere kittens can roar like lions when our children are threatened.

The bone-deep urge to protect our children breeds the king-size fears we acquire as parents. We instinctively know the precious value of our children—some of us had to go through more stress, strain, and strife than we ever thought we could bear to become parents. So we yearn to keep them safe. We'd give just about anything—including our own lives—to keep them safe.

How many of us have tripped with the baby carrier and smashed our own faces into the sidewalk before we let our precious bundle hit the ground? We place their safety above our own. The only trouble is, "safety" suddenly becomes mighty hard to come by. What's safe? The definition seems to change with each passing day.

From the week I discovered I was pregnant, I could find 101 reasons to worry about my little embryo. Down to the *cellular* level. Spinal structure. Brain function. Each set of *how tos* I received (and there seem to be gazillions of those) came with a lethal by-product: *What if I fail to do this?* What if I don't get enough protein in those crucial early weeks? What if I don't bond with him or her at birth? What if I let her suck her thumb too long? What *is that* in his diaper? Will that fourth Tootsie Roll really set him up for a lifelong sugar addiction? Toy swords or no toy swords? White bread or wheat? Pierced ears? Pierced anything else? Car keys! *Prom!*

It feels like the world is out to get us. But it's not, is it? Safe things exist. Safe things abound. Last time I checked, God was still in control. The question, then, that becomes the daily guardian of parents is: What is safe?

Most of us, if we were lucky, felt safe as children. Even if we didn't feel safe all the time, we probably felt generally secure. Now that we are parents, we're all looking for that secret formula that will let us know our children feel the same way. If our childhoods were not good ones and we didn't feel safe as children, we're looking even harder for that secret security formula. We don't want our children to have to go through what we endured. We're determined to improve on the parenting we had.

We've convinced ourselves that there is more at stake now that we are parents. That assumption is not entirely wrong. It's easy to forget, though, that all the strengths we brought through life are still with us. It is just that someone else is now depending on them as well. A small someone who is dependent on our choices, our judgment, our capabilities.

Fear in parenting? How could there not be? It's where we take it from here that matters.

Fear-Facing Questions

Are you a fearful parent? Where would you rate your fear level on a scale of one to ten? Are you happy about how you rate? How would you like things to change? What results would such a change bring in your life and the lives of your children?

Fear Fighter

The most basic fear fighter of all is to recognize that fear is a fact of life. Fighting fear does not mean removing fear; it means no longer being ruled by fearful behavior. Don't seek to remove fear; seek to tame it.

<u>Faith-Finding Verse</u>

Fear not.

(No less that sixty-five separate references: Gen. 15:1; Exod. 20:20; Deut. 1:21; Josh. 8:1; Judges 4:18; Ruth 3:11; 1 Sam. 12:20; 1 Kings 17:13; 1 Chron. 28:20; Ps. 64:4; Isa. 7:4; Jer. 40:9; 46:27; Lam. 3:57; Dan. 10:12, 19; Joel 2:21; Zech. 8:13; Mal. 3:5; Matt. 1:20; 10:28; 28:5; Luke 1:13; 2:10; 5:10; 8:50; 12:7; 12:32; John 12:15; Acts 27:24; Rev 1:17)

Challenge 2:
We Fear We Lack Courage

Fear—the Gift Nobody Wants

Fear is not going to go away. Especially not these days; and in reality, not ever. Lately, though, it seems much harder to say, "Everything will be all right"—the mantra of good mothers. But we're moms. We're supposed to be the Everything Is All Right people.

Have you found that not only do big, rational fears challenge us as parents but that a relentless onslaught of small and not-so-small fears unravels our parenting as well? Drug resistance training. Alpha fetal protein tests. X-raying Halloween candy. Rap lyrics. Remedial reading. S.A.T. scores. College tuition costs.

There's no need for fuzzy math here: Parenting = Stuff to Fear. Argh. How can we cope?

Hang on to your Dove bars, ladies; perhaps it's not as bad as we think. In fact, fear has a purpose. Fear, as bestselling author Gavin deBecker so powerfully states in his book *The Gift of Fear*, can be a just that—a "gift."[1] Fear is one of God's carefully designed instincts—one that plays a crucial role in keeping us alive. Fear heightens awareness and analysis. Fear jump-starts chemical reactions that increase our strength, stamina, and ability to respond.

Fear is also part of stepping out of our comfort zones to expand ourselves and our abilities. Few things produce results more than fear, risk, and tension. God has sent many men and women into situations that seemed like certain doom—just dripping with scary stuff. For that experience, those faithful people earned memories of God's extraordinary power and protection that made them fear-less, outstanding servants of God. Emotionally and spiritually, fear can strengthen our trust in our Lord, our abilities, our family, and our capacity to cope.

The bottom line is that fear is the necessary element to courage. If we want to raise courageous children, we have to find a way to be courageous parents. Like nutrition, discipline, math, and morals, courage in the face of fear is a necessary ingredient in our role as God's chosen molders and caregivers for our little ones. It's far better to look at it that way than to pretend we ought not to be afraid.

> *Like nutrition, discipline, math, and morals, courage in the face of fear is a necessary ingredient in our role as God's chosen molders and caregivers for our little ones.*

We ought to be afraid, but only some. Left uncontrolled or unattended, fear can have terrible consequences. It can paralyze us, robbing us of our freedom and the needed opportunities of risk and challenge. It can cause us to overcompensate, skewing our wise choices into unwise ones. Fear can make us irrational, even dangerous.

So where's the balance? When does caution cross the fine line into smothering? When does prudence become paralyzing? It seems an impossible feat to balance fear's advantages and disadvantages.

That's why parenting feels like a high-wire act. It's important to know how high off the ground we are. How far can we fall? Yet if we look down, we may freeze in fear and never make it across the wire to the other side. Still, it's possible—even probable with the right tools and training—to make it to the other side. Repeatedly.

So, as far as I'm concerned, moms are up on the tightrope. Calling parenting a high-wire act is a powerful metaphor that gives me strength. It helps me remember that walking across a wire *is possible*. Scary, risky, but possible.

As a point of reference, I went out and got sufficient training to actually walk across a wire. Yes, really. Now I'll admit it was only two or three feet off the ground—the high-wire equivalent of training wheels. But it was an extraordinary experience full of interesting people, surprises, and potent lessons. Basic as my training was, it wasn't easy, it took far longer than I expected, and it hurt. Still, it was incredibly cool. I felt a tremendous sense of accomplishment when I made it across my tiny, low wire. Amazing and energizing. Allie Pleiter, mild-mannered housewife, low-wire artist-in-training. Even my kids were impressed (and ain't *that* worth something!).

Besides my dignity, I didn't take a real risk. What I did was fun and interesting, but it wouldn't make much of a circus act. Circus acts—rather like parenting—are defined by raising the stakes. A mere swing becomes a trapeze once you raise it high enough. The achievable novelty of the low wire becomes the death-defying tension of the high wire once you put it forty feet in the air.

Even if every day of parenting isn't a life-and-death situation, it often feels like it. For that matter, many days parenting feels very much like a three-ring circus. Who am I kidding? It feels like an *eight*-ring circus!

So I've decided that facing my fears as a parent is a high-wire act. I'm trembling, but I'm going to make it across. Let's break this amazing feat down into each of its components and see what lessons are to be learned. Each place on the journey, each element of the high-wire experience, has a parental counterpart.

You don't need to join the circus to benefit from the high wire. You just need to keep reading.

Fear-Facing Questions

What parts of parenting feel most "scary, risky, but possible" to you? Do you know why? How would your parenting change in that area if you could reduce your fear?

Fear Fighter

Fight against feeling alone in any fear you have. Talk about it with good friends and other mothers. Knowing you are not alone in any given worry will help you take comfort and find courage in battling that fear.

Faith-Finding Verse

The Lord is my light and my salvation—whom shall I fear? The Lord is the stronghold of my life—of whom shall I be afraid?

Psalm 27:1

Challenge 3:
We Fear When We Lose Perspective
The Overactive Mommy Harm Alarm

When harm befalls our children—no matter how it came upon them—we feel like *we've* harmed them. I've talked to hundreds of mothers who can recall an early parenting "mistake" in vivid detail. Just the other night, my friend Laura told me about a memory she has of walking on the seashore. Really, how picture-postcard can you get? Mom and kiddies strolling hand-in-hand along the beach looking for shells. Where's the harm in that?

Laura described the scene quite differently. She told me how she was too close to the large waves, how she turned her back for a second to look up the shore and was struck by a wave she didn't see coming. The undertow sucked her smallest son out of her hand, and for the space of a minute—which she remembers as feeling like hours—he was lost in the foam. She found him by the bright green of his swimsuit.

Laura's son is fine. Her children are in college now, having faced and met a thousand challenges to their safety over the years. Happy and healthy men, devoid of any water phobias whatsoever. No harm had been done. Yet Laura can still recall that scene down to the last excruciating detail. She got chills right there in front of me just telling the story about how that one event gave her a constant fear for her own potential carelessness as a mother. How she feared at any second she could overlook one variable, and something tragic could be the result. How easily any mother can slip and let harm sneak through.

Each one of us has a story like that or are about to gain a story like that. The realization of our imperfect-at-best protection comes to every mother on earth. Mine came when Amanda was a baby.

I was a working mom then, and my favorite accessory—as a matter of fact it was closer to a trademark for me than an accessory—was a chrome briefcase. This attaché was sleek and oh-so-cool. I loved this case. People knew me by it. It looked like something James Bond would carry, not some lady with a diaper bag on the other shoulder, which, of course, was part of the attraction.

One morning as we were just finishing our contortions of getting both of us into coats, carriers, and snowsuits, I was pulling on the final collection of bags (lunch bag, brief-case, diaper bag, shopping bag with extra stuff, etc.). Duly burdened, I bent down to pick up Amanda's carrier off the foyer floor so we could head out the door.

If you've been strung like a Christmas tree with a half dozen bags like most moms, you know the posture. You hoist the bags over your shoulder, tilting them onto your back so you can bend over. I'm betting you can already see this one coming. As I bent over, the collection of bags slid off my back and came swinging down toward Amanda, chrome briefcase in the lead. Yes, that's right, a metal object was now heading in the direction of my precious daughter. Now I'm struck by the poignancy of that favorite object being the method of destruction in this instance, but such deep thoughts were far from my brain at the time.

What filled my brain at that moment was panic. As I felt the baggage sliding off my back, time slowed down in special-effects-Hollywood-action-flick style, allowing me to experience each heart-wrenching split second to the fullest. I watched my hands shoot over to protect Amanda's body, felt everything I had been carrying slide off in a dozen directions, heard my voice cry out in fear. I watched, in disastrous detail, as the metal briefcase catapulted toward her head despite my every effort to stop it. I was almost able to deflect it, and it mostly struck her carrier seat just to the right of her head, but not before giving both her cheek and my hand a considerable whack.

You can tell me it could have been much worse. You can tell me that I protected my daughter and no serious injury befell her. But to me that memory will never be anything other than *the first time I let harm befall my child.* I had failed to protect her. *My* choice of baggage had done *her* harm. I think I cried for twenty minutes straight—certainly longer than Amanda wailed at the bump on her cheek. Then there was the week or so she bore the bruise, and it seemed like everyone on God's green earth asked me how she got it. Amanda has had other accidents, has been to the emergency room for stitches, and has survived some rather nasty scrapes, but I remember this incident with far more emotional strife than any other.

I use both these moments as examples precisely because they are so extreme. Airborne attachés and child-sucking waves aside, they are instances in which much more harm befell a mother's spirit than her children. In truth, I did not harm my child. I did not hurl the briefcase at her with malicious intent. And Laura did not let her toddler wander into the waves, nor did she toss him in for the sport of it.

But yes, both might have been prevented. It certainly felt like I ought to have prevented it. My mind not only instantly concocted a dozen ways I could have prevented it from happening but also created two dozen scenarios of what *could have* happened. Everything from broken jaws to dislodged eyeballs—the ferocity of the damage grew with my potent imagination. For the next week I would scarcely carry a wallet and her in the same trip, much less the full regalia of baggage needed by mothers of young children.

Did Laura or I blow our "failure" experiences out of proportion? It's hard to say. Proportion doesn't come easily to parents. Our perspective seems to ebb and flow by the hour. Some of the things we think are nothing turn into full-blown crises: "Mom *how could you* throw away that stick? It's my action magic mega-wand!" But just as many things we are sure will be disastrous end up mere trifles: "So I missed my bus stop. She just drove around and dropped me off at the end of the route. It's no big deal." Never mind that we were standing on the corner, wailing into our cell phones, sure our little second grader was hot and scared and crying all alone on that big, lonely bus.

Perspective seems to be fear's most powerful antidote. That's not good, because we as parents are in mighty short supply of perspective. How on earth are we to know what's worth worrying about? What isn't worth worrying about? It feels as though even once we figure out an answer, it can change in a heartbeat. I mean, really, who of us even gave a second thought to opening our mail before September 2001? We were too busy worrying about kidnappers at the mall and drug dealers on the playground. Choking hazards and toy recalls. Missing those crucial teachable moments. Whether our car seats were strapped in correctly.

> *Perspective seems to me to be fear's most powerful antidote. That's not good, because we as parents are in mighty short supply of perspective.*

Now fear seems an irremovable part of our lives. The post-September 11 world feels as if it contains things to be afraid of like never before. We've all received a monumental reminder of hatred's capacity for harm when the attacks on New York City and Washington D.C. were perpetrated. The year 2003 found our nation at war with young men and women dying as a result—not to mention more civilian casualties than we may ever know. The world is holding its collective breath, waiting for SARS to return this coming winter. We are thinking maybe we ought to wear surgical masks next time we fly. Even those Y2K supplies we were urged to buy didn't have the anxiety of the duct tape and plastic sheeting we were asked to buy in 2003 in preparation for the threat of bioterrorism.

In today's world, it seems there is almost too much to fear.

Rest assured, Mom, you're not oversensitive, you're not making mountains out of molehills. This is a scary time. But Franklin D. Roosevelt had it right: "There is nothing to fear but fear itself."[2] Our parents, grandparents, and generations of parents before us have dealt with fears and obstacles—many of them far greater than the challenges we face today. What sustained them? What did they learn? How did they maintain that perspective? What lessons does God have for us as we face our fears?

There are no easy answers. The solutions and situations will look different for each individual. But they are available. It's up to us to find them. My prayer is that this book will lead you to yours.

Fear-Facing Questions

Do you have a memory like the wave or briefcase story—a close call that made you second-guess your skills? Why has that single incident created such a powerful memory? Do you feel your parenting would be better or worse if you did not have that memory?

Fear Fighter

Remember that generations of parents have dealt with fears—many of them much stronger fears than ones you face now. Ask God to adjust your perspective, reminding you of those who've parented through war, illness, or loss and helping you remember that good parenting is possible even in the worst of circumstances.

Faith-Finding Verse

The Lord watches over you—the Lord is your shade at your right hand; the sun will not harm you by day, nor the moon by night. The Lord will keep you from all harm—he will watch over your life; the Lord will watch over your coming and going both now and forevermore.

Psalm 121:5–8

The Amazing Feats of Daring Me?

No one wants fear to hang around. No one craves living in fear. We all seek comfort, peace of mind, and the reassurance that we're going about this parenting feat in the right way. Anxiety is not a virtue. If fear is a gift, it's a gift *no one* wants to receive.

So how do we journey from fear to courage? How do we, mild-mannered mothers that we are, get from one side of this high wire to the other?

The secret is training. In this sense, the gift of fear is no different than the gift of a talent. We are all, by our created nature, "gifted" in fear. Okay, some of us would argue that we're *exceptionally* gifted in this area. It's important to remember, then, that just the possession of a gift or talent is rarely enough to use it wisely. Training is vital.

I couldn't have just walked into the Actors Gymnasium in Evanston, Illinois, and strolled across the wire. Even if I have the desire, even if I understand the value, I simply haven't the *skill*. I needed training.

Consider this book your training for courage. The virtue of fearlessness is a myth—fear should always be with us. As a matter of fact, someone devoid of fear—not just on the high wire but anywhere in the world—is dangerous! There is a military classification known as "NAFOD," which stands for "no apparent fear of death." NAFODs are highly dangerous people—nearly unstoppable weapons capable of great destruction because they have no fear.

No, fear is not bad. It simply must be met with courage.

For the rest of this book, we're going to break down the journey from fear to courage into a metaphorical high-wire act. Each element of the high-wire walk becomes its own unique lesson to us—the wire, the steps, the balance pole, the altitude, and so on. We'll examine each one to soak in all that it has to teach.

Along the way we'll get some expert training. In addition to the coaching of my high-wire teachers, I called upon a group of licensed mental-health professionals to lend their expertise to this journey. Drs. Todd Cartmell, E. Maurlea Babb, and Paulette Toburen, joined by therapist Jenny Gresko, all spoke with me at length about the stories shared in this book and the role fear plays in our lives. All of them are parents (and one is even a grandparent) and have lived the daily challenges of parenting. They offer us practical guidance, sound strategies, and professional perspective. Take heart, ladies, we've got some great teachers up here with us.

Are you ready? Of course not, who is?

That, I'm guessing, is part of the lesson.

Ladies and gentlemen, children of all ages, I direct your attention to high above the center ring . . .

Chapter 2

THE PLATFORM

*"I'm afraid I can't do it. I fear I'll snap and lose
my sanity and not be able to take care of my family.
Or my anger and frustration will pull my children down
and drown their spirits."*

*"I'm afraid my children will feel the same way
about me that I feel about my mom."*

"I fear I'm passing on my poor self-image to my daughters."

*"I'm so scared that I will die and there is no one
who could ever replace me."*

How Did We Get Here?

Every journey starts somewhere. In high-wire walking the starting platform is where aerialists center themselves, assess the present situation, and make final adjustments based on temperature, lighting, injury, noise, etc. It is where they get mind and body ready to walk the wire. We need to do the same as parents.

Like every other step in our journey, the platform has things to teach us. About who we are now. About the past we bring to this place. About our viewpoint and our individual struggles. About taking a breath and taking a moment to prepare.

When we face a threat or challenge, it's wise to take a moment and soak in the view, ponder the feat ahead of us, and assess the tools at our disposal. Where are we and what are we facing? What strengths do we bring? What weaknesses do we have for which we need to compensate? Are there real-life equivalents of a circus's bright lights and loud noises that might prove harmful distractions? Taking the time to ask—and answer—these tough questions helps us succeed.

I know what you're thinking. You're wondering if stopping to take a good long look around is really a wise idea. At first it just seems like a surefire recipe to send our pulses soaring. It might feel like staring downward just after everyone's told you, "Don't look down!" High-wire walking, though, is no stroll in the park. It has dangers and variables and any number of issues that command our respect and attention. Taking stock of our state is a far wiser choice than plowing through a challenge without any forethought. We

need to think the situation through, and the platform—
however nerve-racking—is the place to do just that.

In the next few chapters we'll examine fears and threats
that hinge on how we got up here to
walk this parenting tightrope in the first
place. We'll examine situational fears.
We'll explore fears sprung from emotional baggage, from personality traits,
or from the scars left from previous
experiences. Why? Because knowing
who we are tells us a whole lot about
how best to cope.

> *Taking stock of our state is a far wiser choice than plowing through a challenge without any forethought.*

Sure, it's high. The view, though, will knock your socks off.

So take a deep breath and come on up to the high-wire
platform, my sisters in shivers. Take a good long look
around. You may learn a lot from what you see.

Challenge 1:
We Fear the Unknown
Why You Probably Won't Ever Drop Your Newborn

"I'm not sure I can pull off this parenting thing!" Ever thought that? Relax, girl, every mom in the universe is raising her hand right alongside you.

From the first day that child enters our lives, the consequences of our failure loom large. We jump into parenthood with no more training than a lucrative babysitting career, or, if we're lucky, a couple of children in our lives such as nieces or nephews. Most of us quickly catch on, though, that such things are nowhere near enough preparation. There are no real rehearsals for parenting. We can watch others parent and get a grip on the essential skills, but in large part the full-time parenting gig is *on-the-job-training* frighteningly devoid of coaches and spotters.

Every parent suffers the same culture shock of those first few weeks at home. *Bam!* We're parents. Thrust onto this high-wire platform and staring at the death-defying feat of parenting. We've looked at it before, probably even longed for it. Labor takes hours, adoption or infertility can take years, but none of that makes you a *parent*. A lifetime of responsibility lands in your arms in a matter of seconds. Holding your new child, grafting her new life irrevocably into your own life, *this* is when parenting starts. And the task before us looks downright impossible.

My husband, Jeff, and I were the most book-laden, educated, planned-out parents on earth. I had spreadsheets, outlines, lists, and notebooks. I didn't just have a pregnancy,

I *managed* my pregnancy. I had every detail laid out in astounding order.

None of that meant a blessed thing the first night we brought our daughter, Amanda, home. Three weeks early. After a wicked labor and an unplanned C-section.

I remember my terror-filled stupor that first night. *I'm a mother. She's home now. There's a baby. In our house.* Sure, we'd spent months preparing. We had all the latest paraphernalia. It all matched our carefully chosen color scheme. We'd strapped her into the spanking new car seat and oh so cautiously drove her home for the first time. The pristine containers of baby powder, ointment, and wipes stood in near-military splendor on our changing table. The nightlight and adorable linens were enjoying their first uses. Our brand new baby daughter had been asleep for a few hours, and things were just starting to feel normal around the edges.

Then we tried to sleep ourselves.

Desperate as I was to sleep in my own bed, exhausted and still recovering from the surgery, I couldn't nod off. I was filled with fear that I wouldn't hear her cries for help—even with the aid of a monitor turned up so high I could probably hear her blink. Fearful I wouldn't know how to help her now that those nice, calm maternity ward nurses were far away. Fearful, even, that she wouldn't wake up at all but die of some horrible, unknown ailment in her sleep. Frighteningly aware of my inability to protect her every moment, but stressfully aware that something could happen to her at any moment.

Like women have for centuries, my brain began concocting dozens of neglectful parent scenarios. Allie Pleiter, the March cover girl for *Bad Mothers Monthly.* Lying in my bed, wide-eyed in the dark, straining to hear each tiny breath, I second-guessed every grunt and coo. I bet there's not a woman among you who doesn't have the same memory, no matter when or how your children came into your life.

> *Like women have for centuries, my brain began concocting dozens of neglectful parent scenarios. Allie Pleiter, the March cover girl for Bad Mothers Monthly.*

I was scared out of my jammies that night because I had convinced myself that the consequences of my incompetence were now life and death. I wasn't entirely wrong; they were, to some degree. I am fully aware that there are parents out there who have been awakened to heart-wrenchingly tragic circumstances. Children *have* died silently in the middle of the night. I wasn't wrong to worry. If something dire did happen to Amanda, it was very important that I recognize it quickly and act appropriately.

Years later, it is still a life-and-death situation. The stakes are still high. But I'm no longer as frightened of sleeping through the night (as a matter of fact, I crave it!). The reason seems obvious, but it is actually a powerful truth: I have experience now.

On that first night I brought Amanda home, you couldn't convince me I was capable of hearing her in the night because I was missing the essential solution of experience. Only getting through my first night would give me the ability to know I could do it. Being woken in the middle of the night is one of the regularities of parenthood. In itself, it involves no special skill. We all have the capacity to do it: thrusting your feet out of those nice, toasty covers to fumble on the nightstand for your glasses and shrug yourself into your bathrobe as you shuffle down the dark hall toward the nightlight glow of the nursery. Let's face it: For the new parent, sleep deprivation isn't a symptom, it's a *lifestyle*.

Only a bunch of nights would teach me that the consequences of Mandy's night wakenings were far more about nursing and diapers than life and death. Only experience would make it all become very, very ... *groan* ... *yawn* ... ordinary. I interviewed Dr. Todd Cartmell, who is both a clinical child psychologist and a father of two, to gain his insights on the subject of parents and fear. Cartmell told me that competence is the only route to the perspective I needed to assuage my fear. While familiarity may breed contempt in other aspects of life, it breeds comfort for us parents. We need to accumulate what Cartmell calls a "personal bank of evidence" that tells us it will be okay—evidence that would make those nights familiar territory instead of foreign ground. After a dozen years of parenting, being woken up to deal with some nocturnal, child-born crisis is just part of life for me now.

As it turned out, we hardly ever used a monitor after that first night. We learned very quickly that Amanda had lungs—*opera-quality* lungs. We could hear her across the yard, much less across the hall. You couldn't have told me that, though; I had to *learn* it. Like the old "Goin' on a Bear Hunt" song says, "Can't get over it, can't go under it, can't go around it, gotta go *through* it." A million parenting books, even Dr. Spock himself in my living room, would not have done the trick. Only personal, hard evidence would build the competence I needed to fight my fear.

That may sound helpless, but think about the value of this: If I know experience is the only way out of a situation, then I can focus my energy on getting there. There is some comfort in knowing the only solution is simply to *do it*. At least once, more likely a dozen times.

Experience helps with another fear. Despite the fact that if you can carry a glass vase, you can carry a newborn, I've yet to meet the new mother who isn't afraid she'll drop the baby. All that "hold the head, their necks aren't strong enough" makes you nuts, thinking you'll snap their tender little spines if you aren't paying attention. They seem so incredibly fragile, and we're so incredibly scared and tired. But after a month, it's old hat. You carry them instinctively, almost casually. You have experience.

Telling yourself, "Yes, this is scary, but it won't always be this way," is useful. It gives us permission to be afraid but not to be dissuaded. It reminds us that even if we haven't got any evidence in our banks yet, that evidence *is* forthcoming.

> Telling yourself, "Yes, this is scary, but it won't always be this way," is useful. It gives us permission to be afraid but not to be dissuaded.

Many times, though, the evidence is hard to see. That's bad, because if we can't see it, we can't reduce our fear. When that happens, we need to go *looking* for experience. In his excellent layman's guide to cognitive therapy entitled *The Feeling Good Handbook*, Dr. David D. Burns proposes a useful tool called a "Daily Mood Log" to do just that.[3] He suggests that during a stressful time, we keep a daily log of things that make us tense (or any other debilitating emotion, such as sadness or anger) and rate our level of that emotion. It works especially well for fear.

For example, let's look at the first time you have to do all those yucky things to your newborn's umbilical cord. You're certain the viney-looking scab will fall off in your hands and he'll bleed to death because it was, after all, once his major source of blood flow. Your fear rate would probably be in the 90 percent range. The next time you grab that alcohol and cotton swab, you'll have gained the knowledge that you both can actually survive this little medical maintenance, and your fear rate might drop to 75 percent. You'll miss that drop in fear if you don't stop to recognize it. A Daily Mood Log lets you recognize even small drops in fear. Seeing that progression toward calm will help you find courage. It gives you hard evidence. Chances are your fear will drop with each successive night of your newborn's first week at home. Or Junior's first week at preschool. Or Molly's first stint at summer camp. Or each time you have to administer a complicated new medicine to your child. Any time the only way out is to "just do it."

Recognizing the unfamiliarity of any situation will help us. It shows us that at least *part* of what we fear isn't the threat of the situation itself but just our low competence level. Luckily, our competence level is often within our control. We control it by choosing to gain experience or by choosing to remember that experience is surely on the way.

Fear-Facing Questions

Where is your unfamiliar parenting territory? Once you see it, can you see how it is causing you fear? Where is the "just do it" path to competence? Point it out to yourself and see if that new focus bolsters your courage.

Fear Fighter

Make a Daily Mood Log to keep track of times you face fears based on unfamiliarity. Show yourself, as you chart your fear levels, how experience is building competence to fight your fear.

Faith-Finding Verse

Even though I walk through the valley of the shadow of death, I will fear no evil, for you are with me; your rod and your staff, they comfort me.

Psalm 23:4

Challenge 2:
Emotional Baggage Breeds Our Fears
Why Oreos Are Not Deadly

When I began asking women about their fears as mothers, I often received some version of the following answer: "I'm afraid they'll turn out like me." *Whoa, Nellie.* That's some heavy baggage to lug into the nursery. Parenting is a scary place to hang a fragile self-esteem.

Family therapist Dr. E. Maurlea Babb, another member of my panel of experts for this book, told me that individuals get over one thousand mental messages a day—from media, people, emotions, and internal and external factors. Thanks to those numerous daily messages—many of which are negative whether they're true or not—many of us fear the bad example we're convinced we set.

Why? Because women are creatures of comparison. Women are, by nature, self-examining. We endlessly dissect our character, our nature, our relationships. We analyze everything. All the time. It may be born of the desire to improve, but it all too often leaves a shredded self-esteem in its wake. Ask a woman to name her faults, and she'll often ask how much time you have.

Every mother cringes at the prospect of our children learning from the poor example of our own bad habits. If you're the kind of woman who recoils at the phrase, "You're just like your mother" (so often said at the worst possible time by a spouse or sibling), you live in fear of how easily it happens. I know I have several shortcomings I feel nearly helpless to correct. Sure, I'm not really helpless, but I *feel* that way.

A prime recent example is my weight. Like many women, weight has been an issue most of my adult life, since someone flipped that evil hormone switch at around twenty-six and suddenly everything started expanding and heading south. My children see me as (and this is a direct quote) "Mommy shaped." Soft and squishy. Cuddle-ready. I do not share their view; to me it looked like thirty pounds of extra weight, not a walking hug invitation. Yes, I was still within (but admittedly on the upper limits of) a healthy weight for my height. My figure was thinner than many other moms my age. But did I see that? No, I was busy looking at the *other* women. The woman who looks great for her age. The one who *still has a waist*. The one who can wear a tankini without shame.

Why? I think I've figured out part of it. My mother was significantly overweight and suffered health consequences because of it. So I see those thirty pounds as inching me closer (literally) to the problems my mother had, and it makes me *nuts*. When I see even a sliver of its manifestation in my children (who are, by the way, quite lean), the internal fear-guilt mechanism slams into high gear.

You'd think, as a result, that I'd be a nutrition nut. That would be the logical path. But no, ma'am. I go down the *emotionally scenic* route. I draw crazy, illogical, mostly useless conclusions. I'm perhaps too lax on my nutrition rules. Why? Because I'm convinced my mom's rigors (she kept very few sweets in the house because she had no more willpower than I seem to have) made me the sugar junkie I am. I have clear memories of pigging out on sweets at other kids' houses because there weren't any at home.

So you see, if I don't *deny* my kids Oreos, then they won't *crave* Oreos, then they won't *binge* on Oreos, but still right now they're eating *too many* Oreos—you get the picture. I fear for their weight not because *they* have a problem (trust me, they don't) but because I think *I* have a problem they'll inherit. How much sense does *that* make?

I didn't figure this out until I realized it wasn't actually bad nutrition or even obesity I feared. What I truly feared was the sense of helplessness—a supposed genetic flaw that rendered me defenseless against the struggles my mother had. The key for me was to realize that fear for what it was: a lie. Even if I have a genetic predisposition to "Mommy shape," and a nasty cardiac family heritage to boot, *I can control* most of the other major risk factors. I am not helpless. Once I recognized that lie for what it was, an amazing thing began to happen. Nailing the true source of my fear gave me new confidence and motivation to exercise that elusive control. I began to prove to myself that I wasn't really helpless. I joined a weight-loss program and have shed twenty of those pounds since I came to that vital realization. That's the power identifying your true fear can have.

This is only one example. Your life hosts different fears, different lies. That is why we must spend time looking our fear *in the face*. Spend some time examining, thinking, and talking to people who love you about what it is you fear. Can you clarify or pinpoint what it is you are truly afraid of? You will know it deep in your bones when you hit it— and it will contain great power for you to harness. Isn't that worth a long, nerve-racking look around?

Not that such deep truths come out of hiding easily. If you've done some examining and you're still stuck, or if you're feeling just vague and unfocused fear, there are strategies to help you identify the true core of your fear. Dr. Burns recommends a rather silly but effective exercise of drawing a stick figure.[4] That's right, whip out a piece of paper and draw a little stick mom. Put a frown on her face. Give her a bad hair day. Make her look scared. Make her "Mommy shaped" if you need to (in my case her stick figure would just make me feel worse). Ask her what she's really afraid of. Then draw a little cartoon dialogue balloon next to her face and fill it in. Write down the first thing that comes to mind. Let her tell you what's scaring her. Yes, I know it sounds ridiculous, and even Dr. Burns says he doesn't understand why this is so effective, but it really works. Draw a couple of stick figures, asking the same question, and you'll be amazed what pops out of paper Mama's mouth. A phrase will just jump out of your pencil, and you'll know that's the real problem. Then, and only then, can you craft a real solution.

I know this absurd-sounding exercise works because that's how I pinpointed my weight issue. And you'd be amazed at the power it gave me. For the first time in decades I actually *am* the weight on my driver's license!

Fear-Facing Questions

Where do you feel helpless as a parent? As a wife? As a woman? Can you take a long look and identify what emotional baggage is fueling that fear?

Fear Fighter

Draw a silly cartoon stick figure of yourself and ask her why she's afraid. Do it over and over, without editing your responses, until you hit the true issue. Call it for the lie it is, if appropriate. Let the power of identifying that true fear help bolster you to craft a solution.

Faith-Finding Verse

Then you will know the truth, and the truth will set you free.

John 8:32

Challenge 3:
We Fear What We're Taught to Fear
Why Panic Buttons Abound

Life gets sticky when we realize we bring our own childhoods and our parents' view of life into our parenthood. How we—and those around us—view certain aspects of life has a tremendous effect on what we fear and how much we fear it. We learned from my Oreo obsession that our fear baggage often leads us to complicated, counterproductive emotional cycles. These cycles can ripple out in regrettable ways to our family as well.

Take my friend. She's a great mother, a consummate planner, a woman who's handled much of what life has thrown at her with determination and persistence (and believe me, life has thrown some doozies her way). If competence fights fear, this woman has serious ammunition. She's talented, organized, and has a dozen strong reasons to be saying, "I know what to do." You'd think.

This strong, competent woman called me once in utter terror of a simple medical procedure. Actually, it wasn't even a procedure, just a test. She'd been experiencing some pain, and a doctor ordered a relatively ordinary test to help identify what was causing the pain.

I could see that. She couldn't. By the time she called me, she had herself terminally ill, leaving traumatized children behind to face the world without their mother. She'd not envisioned illness or even disability. No, she jumped straight to her own impending demise. Pain = cancer = death. End of equation.

I know none of you are "hrumphing" (you know "hrumphing"—that sound men make when they think we're being ridiculous?) because *we've all done it.* I'm sure there are men who blow things out of proportion, but from my experience it seems to be a particularly female talent. Our relational gifts lead us to draw things out to relational consequences. When women talk to me about their fears of dying, it's never in terms of the end of their own life. No, we're all worried about leaving *motherless children,* about not seeing them grow up. We're envisioning them on the therapist's couch moaning their abandonment issues because we up and died on them at a crucial age.

My friend had some hefty baggage pulling her down this path. She'd lost her father to cancer and has lived a lifetime under the shadow of her mother's fear of cancer. Many of us now in our thirties and forties have parents who still think of cancer as a death sentence. It's not nowadays in many cases, but our parents still think of it that way. My own mother had trouble even uttering the word. Thirty years of alarmist, cautionary thinking is hard to undo. My friend's history of cancer concerns and years of listening to her mother's worry pulled her under. She had, quite naturally, allowed her emotional baggage to blow the situation way out of proportion.

> When women talk to me about their fears of dying, it's never in terms of the end of their own life. No, we're all worried about leaving motherless children.

Women can easily take an event and lay out multiple disastrous consequences because we have the gift of seeing connections in things. Take our fear button, press it, and watch us explode in eleven different directions. Logic isn't even part of the picture. Every woman has one or more issues like my friend's cancer thing; one tiny problem and we've blown it into a tornado of fear.

Now don't get me wrong. I'm not one for blaming parents, even when they've hoisted a load of baggage on us and we're left coping with the burden. No one's parents sit around and think up ways to rack up a life-long therapy bill. My friend's mother had legitimate fears. She'd lived through the death of a loved one to cancer, and that would skew *anyone's* point of view. She didn't set out to give her daughter "issues."

> Take our fear button, press it, and watch us explode in eleven different directions.

Parenting is just plain hard. Parents are human, and mistakes happen. Less-than-wise choices are made. But I believe it's far better to spend our energy on finding ways to lift the load of baggage than whining about how it got there in the first place.

The key to lifting that load is to realize that logic has "left the building." Panic buttons defy logic. Any medical doctor or statistician could have laid out fairly comfortable odds to my friend that she was not in a life-threatening situation. Not only that, but I knew that this friend had already endured some hefty issues in her life, and even if a medical crisis was about to arrive, she had the fortitude to get through it. As you can imagine, all of these arguments did nothing to assuage my friend's fear.

Why? Because *fears that come from illogical bases can't be logically argued away*. That doesn't make them silly or small. In fact, it makes them more powerful. Fears that come from baggage aren't based on logic—in fact, fears are *feelings*, which places them out of the logical realm by definition.

After about a day of trying to calmly talk my friend out of her fear, I realized that was not going to work. Like the Oreo dilemma in challenge 2, we needed to discover the true nugget of what was making her so scared. It wasn't the test; it wasn't any of the six or seven possible outcomes of the test; it was that *cancer* was one of the possible outcomes—

even though it was only about 8 to 10 percent possible. In her case, even 1 percent would have been enough to kindle the terror. Armed with that information, she could take whatever steps she could to ensure a test result ruling out cancer got to her as fast as possible. She could also make her best attempt at distracting her mind during the weekend's wait for the test to take place. But the best course of action was telling her doctors that cancer was an emotionally charged issue for her, and she needed it ruled out immediately if possible.

Once the doctors understood, they were able to tell her cancer was not a possibility within minutes after the test was conducted. Her fear level went down, her brain cleared a bit, and she could be a helpful, calm patient in determining what the real reasons were behind the pain.

My friend is fine now. And perhaps she's a bit wiser in recognizing what history can do to our perspective.

My history, for example, bequeathed me a bone-deep fear of the dentist. I've come to realize, though, that it's not dental care or even drilling I fear, it's *novocaine*. Yes, you heard me—I'm afraid of a painkiller. Go figure. Like I said, panic buttons defy logic. For many years, rather than face the novocaine needle, I would endure fillings without it (ugh!), imbedding my fingernails in chair arms. I don't blink an eye at other kinds of shots, but you come at me with that silver novocaine needle, and I go ballistic. It will never make sense.

The good news is, though, that it doesn't have to make sense. You can't rationalize a panic button—distraction and reassurance are your best tools here. Once I told my dentist about my high voltage "novaphobia," we could work together to find a solution. And that solution does *not* include listing all of novocaine's nice qualities or how safe it is. None of that logical stuff would help. Instead, now he does several things to distract me while it's being administered;

he administers it as early in my visit as possible so I don't spend the first part of the visit freaking out over the impending novocaine; he administers it very carefully; and he reminds me each time I visit that he remembers my fear.

> The good news is, though, that it doesn't have to make sense. You can't rationalize a panic button—distraction and reassurance are your best tools here.

Despite some searching, I've not yet been able to identify what or who in my history gave this fear to me. I'm not sure it will matter, for I've discovered that sometimes simply finding the panic button in a cloud of fear is solution enough. I don't need to know how it got there. I'm just learning how *not to press it*. As a result, I'm actually much calmer when facing the dentist chair now. Not calm, but calmer.

When facing a fear that seems blown out of proportion to the actual facts at hand (which, when you think about it, may be 90 percent of fears), take a look around. Is it the whole situation you fear? Or is there a panic button in there somewhere?

If the facts don't warrant the fear, something or someone gave you that fear. Sometimes if you can root out the source of that fear and identify the person who passed it on to you (notice I said "identify," not "blame"), you can nail down the real problem. You can see if circumstances—valid or otherwise—skewed that person's viewpoint. *And you can decide you no longer wish to agree*. I'm not saying you'll suddenly transform into a bastion of calm, but you will be harnessing the power of truth to help you on your way to courage. And that is power indeed.

Fear-Facing Questions

What fears do you remember from growing up? Are there trials your family faced that have given you a few inherited panic buttons? What's the truth behind them?

Why do you think knowing that will help you find the courage you need?

Fear Fighter

Once you've uncovered your panic button, toss out the useless rationalizations you have used to fight that fear. They've probably never helped anyway. How, instead, can you distract yourself? What can reassure you in this situation? Make yourself a "distraction and reassurance" plan. It will help far better than any stack of facts.

Faith-Finding Verse

Even in darkness light dawns for the upright.... He will have no fear of bad news; his heart is steadfast, trusting in the Lord. His heart is secure, he will have no fear; in the end he will look in triumph on his foes.
Psalm 112:4, 7–8

Challenge 4:
Our Personalities Bring Fears
Why Pink Ketchup Isn't a Risk for Everyone

New isn't always scary. Our children may have a completely different tolerance for the unknown than we do. Some children are daunted by new things; others live easily with change. My daughter does not welcome the new and different. My son, like me, seems to thrive on change.

My basic instincts for fighting fear rarely work for my daughter because we process the unknown differently. When I forget that, I hamper my ability to let experience be our teacher and tool for getting over fear.

As we respect—and challenge—our own innate response to new situations, we must catch ourselves before we project them onto our children. Are you likely to overcome a fear by thrusting yourself tough-love style into the situation so you "get over it?" Or is that likely to exacerbate the situation?

I'm reminded of the swimming pool. Getting into the pool usually comes in two schools of thought: all at once or a little bit at a time. Think about it: If I am a "little bit" kind of person, will I teach my son to be wary of the water if I squelch his desire to dive right in? Provided safety concerns are met, aren't I better off letting him get in using his own style?

> My basic instincts for fighting fear rarely work for my daughter because we process the unknown differently. When I forget that, I hamper my ability to let experience be our teacher and tool for getting over fear.

Risk reared its head at our house one day in a most unusual manner. My children were wildly delighted when I brought home ketchup in a "Mystery Color" bottle. The thought sort of made me ill—I'm a red-is-the-only-color-ketchup-should-come-in kind of gal. I don't even care for some of the colors Kool-Aid comes in these days (did God really create us to drink anything bright blue?). Since ketchup does not constitute a staple of my diet (as opposed to my offspring, for whom it is close to a vegetable), I found it fun in a sick kind of way. It was a risk I could take because the stakes were not very high for me.

My kids, however, found this a daunting prospect. What would come out of the bottle and onto their chicken nuggets for the next few weeks? What would be the color of the *must-have* condiment on their table? I was vastly entertained by how high the stakes were for them. And just as highly entertained by how they coped with the perceived risk.

CJ, my son, felt comfortable waiting until the proper ketchup-recipient-food found its way onto the table. But Mandy, who doesn't take well to change, just *had* to know right away what the color was. In fact, even before I got the rest of the groceries unpacked, she had pulled out the bottle and was dismantling the vacuum seal so that she could peer inside.

It was a microcosm of the fear-risk scenario. CJ's experience bank could be just fine with "I have an idea what to do." He could risk the unknown and its ramifications easily, even though he is far more the ketchup lover in our house. He was comfortable with the high stakes of wondering if his ketchup would be teal, orange, or pink (the actual choices!). Mandy, on the other hand, wasn't comfortable leaving the risk out there to pick at her curiosity—even though the stakes were not as high. Mandy is the kind of child who needs to be able to say, "I know *exactly* what to do." So she pulled it open right away and found out we'd be living with pink ketchup.

What's the point? Mandy knew—even unconsciously and even about ketchup—what stressed her out, and she did what she could about it. If you don't like fear and risk, actively seek ways to solve the little risk factors you can control. Save your coping skills for the big stuff—stuff you can't control when you need all your wits about you. If you're not a risk taker, save your coping for parenthood and stay out of the stock market. Confirm your hotel reservations with your credit card. Get a fixed rate mortgage. Buy only red ketchup, or take the top off the minute you get home. Sure it's a silly example, but sometimes the silly examples are the best teachers.

Let's take a slightly more grown-up example. I can tolerate quite high levels of risk in many situations, but I just hate to take connecting flights. I'll pay the extra money every time in order to take a nonstop flight. It's not because I hate flying; it's because I found I *obsess* about missing my connection.

I came close to ruining our recent family vacation—or at least getting it off to a very sour start—because I would not stop worrying about whether or not we'd make our connection. We'd finally earned enough frequent flier miles for the whole family to fly to San Francisco *free*, and I ruined it by freaking out over making the connecting flights.

Way to go, Mom. Surefire way to make those happy family memories.

I asked every person in a uniform what we should do if we missed our connection. I held up lines and exasperated flight attendants. I spent a perfectly enjoyable—and did I mention *free?*—flight worrying about something over which I had no control. We were on vacation. We had no set schedule. Life would not come to an end if we arrived in San Francisco several hours late.

My husband, Jeff, was getting rather annoyed at my fixation on this tiny detail. For those few hours, *everybody* paid for my fear.

Sure it's probably worth a good look some day at the emotional reasons for my connecting flight hysteria, but really, aren't I just better off *recognizing* that I'll be calmer on a direct flight? Isn't it worth it to my family and me if I simply *remove* that stress from the picture? The simple fact is that our family vacation trips should include only non-stop flights. That's not bad; that's not caving to my character flaws. It's simply removing stresses I can control so I can save my coping strength for the ones I can't control.

Risk is a fact of life. Some risks—and the fear they produce—cannot be removed. Other risks—and the fears *they* produce—can be removed. To recognize fear's power is not cowardice, it's wisdom. In fighting fear, as in living life, it's always best to choose your battles wisely.

Fear-Facing Questions

What do you feel is your level of risk tolerance? How comfortably do you face new or risky situations? What about your husband? Your children? Where do these parent-child combinations work in your favor? Where do they make things worse?

Fear Fighter

If there's a small risk in your life, does it need to be there? Find those little stresses, those smaller fears we all too often dismiss as silly, and see if you can't remove them. Save your fear fighting for the fears *worth* fighting.

Faith-Finding Verse

But now, this is what the Lord says—he who created you, O Jacob, he who formed you, O Israel: "Fear not, for I have redeemed you; I have summoned you by name; you are mine."

Isaiah 43:1

Hanging Out on the Platform

The platform represents the *what* and the *why* of our fears. If we're to find our way to courage, we must spend a little time up here. We need to look around, take in the view, and identify what it is we're truly facing, what it is we truly fear. That takes a bit of time and a big dollop of courage. It also takes recognizing how high up we are. How breathtaking (in the worst sense of the word) this thing called parenting really is. How much baggage we brought up to this platform with us.

If you're living in fear of something, climb up on your personal platform and look around. Yes, you can bring a pint of Super Fudge Chunk up here if you have to. But make sure you stay up here long enough to see what you need to see.

Why bother going to such lengths? Because this high-wire platform is no spacious veranda. We can't pretend we're not really afraid, and we need to know what we're really afraid of. There's not a lot of room for extra stuff up here. While fear can spark genuine concern and preparation, Dr. Babb reminded me fear also has a great capacity for creating denial and inactivity. These are fear's lethal by-products, often making things far worse whether or not we realize it.

No, the platform is necessary because we need to have a long, clear look around. Author Gavin deBecker tells us that the fear intuition is a vital part of a human being's preloaded survival skills. A gift, one I consider given by God, to help us. But we've lost its focus and often try to deny its existence because we see fear as bad and flawed. We think strong people don't feel fear. As he puts it, "Denial is a save-now-pay-later scheme, a contract written entirely in small print, for in the long run, the denying person knows the truth on some level, and it causes a constant low-grade anxiety. Millions of people suffer that anxiety, and denial keeps them from taking action that could reduce the risks (and the worry)."[5]

We're far better off taking the time to prepare on the platform, looking the situation in the face—even if it raises our blood pressure—than giving in to the denial that might tell us everything is perfectly safe. Because the truth is, it isn't perfectly safe. And truth is our best friend up here.

Ah, but there is one truth worth holding onto above all else. One that transforms all of the issues we've discussed. It's the truth that, even without the doctors, books, and everything, we are not up on the platform alone. God is standing here with us, beside us in encouraging companionship. He's also standing below us, arms outstretched in Almighty safety. And he's standing on the other side, beckoning to us, reminding us of all that's worth striving for.

Chapter 3

THE WIRE

"I'm terrified of leaving the children overnight.
I'm afraid if I'm not with them all the time,
something will happen."

"I worry so much about what the kids are doing
when they're not with me."

"I'm afraid of crossing bridges because if we went
off the side I couldn't save all four kids."

"I'm scared that if something really bad happens
to one of my children, I won't be able to handle it."

How Do We Get There from Here?

Now that we've had a good long look around, it's time to step off the platform. Time to begin our journey toward courage. If we look at our high-wire metaphor, our quest for courage becomes the trip across the wire. The death-defying journey from the place we *are* to the place we *want to be*. From the starting platform to the ending platform—across the tightrope. For any high-wire walker, the first step is to ease your toes out over the edge and find the wire.

Where is that wire? Or, perhaps more to our quest, what are we standing on? What's going to get us across this dangerous divide? What is this wire, and how is it going to hold us up?

What is it about this wire that will transform it from a stretch of intertwined steel to the bridge that it must become? Tension. A wire coiled loosely on the ground would do us about as much good up here as a pair of stiletto heels. We need that wire taut if it's going to hold us up. Tension is what enables the wire to do its job—to get us from where we are to where we want to be. We need, then, to *befriend tension*. We need to recognize that, like in the high wire, tension is an integral part of parenting.

Family counselor Jenny Gresko, another member of our expert panel who is also the mother of a middle-school son, encourages her clients to realize that parenting is full of what she terms "irreconcilable tensions"—opposing forces that will never be in harmony. Yet the dual pull of those forces shapes a path for us to deal with a situation.

Fear comes when we assume tension means danger. That's not true. Sure, we'd all like to run from tension because it is never comfortable, but it's actually not the enemy here. If we're looking to master our fear as mothers, then we need to get to the place where we understand that *feeling tension is not the sign of a bad parent but an active one.*

Our path as parents—our wire, as it were—won't always be comfortable. Walking a wire, in case you'd like to know, hurts. A lot. Your feet aren't made to support your entire body weight on a half inch of your sole. Now that's not a pertinent fact in itself, but I learned a useful parenting lesson in that fact. My teacher told me, before my lesson, to bring two pairs of cushy socks because it hurts. I hadn't associated tightrope walking with pain—I figured it was all about balance. I discovered, however, that I was really glad to know to expect it to hurt. Otherwise, I think I would have spent my first lesson being surprised at the pain instead of learning.

We can apply that to our parenthood. We can either let the surprise of the tension distract us so that we learn next to nothing, or we can expect the tension as the indispensable part of parenting that it is.

Come, let's look at this improbable bridge we're walking. Come find out why you can trust it to get you where you need to go.

> If we're looking to master our fear as mothers, then we need to get to that place where we understand that feeling tension is not the sign of a bad parent but an active one.

Challenge 1:
We Fear Letting Our Children Take Risks

Mandy and the No Good Very Bad
Well Maybe Okay Sleepover

If you want to talk fear, you have to talk sleepovers. Those first sleepovers pose big risks for our children. They want to go have fun with their friends, but it seems scary to sleep somewhere other than home. The opposing forces of desired friendship and known comfort knit up their tiny brows in tension.

As parents, we feel twice the risk. Sure, sleepovers are one of those integral parts of childhood. Yet sleepovers also mean letting our children out of our control and placing them smack into someone else's hands. Overnight. In the dark. Without us. Oh my.

Even though Mandy is eleven, I'm still tense the first time my daughter sleeps over at a new house. Especially if I'm not at a perfect comfort level with my knowledge of the family. And really, is perfect even possible? How well do you *ever* know a family? Where's the line between asking if parents will be home to supervise and asking if there are guns kept in the house?

Last year Mandy was invited to what I'll call a "questionable" sleepover. A party organized by a gaggle of fifth grade girls for no other reason than the opportunity to get together and have fun. The stuff of social growth and building lasting friendships that might help Mandy through the rocky shores of middle school. I was delighted that my on-the-shy-side daughter had been in on the plot to make some fun with a group of her peers.

Ah, but it was at the home of a family I didn't know well. Now a playdate at an unfamiliar home isn't much of a risk, but a sleepover seems to raise the stakes. I had visions of crises—social or medical—in the wee hours of the morning. Yet Mandy had taken great pains to let me know far in advance about this date. (In case you don't know, far in advance is highly unusual behavior for a ten-year-old.) She'd reiterated several times how much she wanted to go.

Let her go? Let her grow socially? Let her spend the night in a questionable environment, which might be perfectly okay or perfectly awful? Keep her home as a wise precaution? I wasn't ready to interrogate the parents in question (although perhaps I should have been). Tension. Tension. Neither option made me comfortable. I felt those opposing forces press in on me. I watched my imagination take that tension and twirl it into worst-case scenarios. Drugs. Alcohol. Abuse. Oija boards. Late-night cable television. "I double-dog dare you to drink a cup of Tabasco sauce!" Eek!

I tell you, by the night in question I was one nervous mother. Fearful for my child, nervous that I didn't have enough information to make a wise choice, fearful that my overprotective, CNN-tensed parenting would squelch her social growth. The act of her crawling into a sleeping bag among four other girls was not the source of tension. It was the opposing desires in my own head—the battle between protection and nurture—that created the tension in this situation. I didn't really like either of the choices available to me.

What *was* available to me, though, was the choice in how to react. What I needed was a pathway to trust. I needed to find enough information to enable me to trust in my daughter, my judgment, and this family.

Oh, yeah, like *that'd* be easy. Short of pulling the plug on the whole outing, the only variables over which I had real control were my daughter and myself. While I listened to the tiny voice that said, "Don't let her go," I also focused on the equally tiny voice that said, "It's important to let her go but to go carefully."

Mandy was God's precious creation. I reminded myself that I could trust God to protect her when I couldn't. I reminded myself of all the times Mandy had shown excellent judgment. She was ten years old, and she had her head on as straight as it gets at that age. She is cautious and analytical by nature—by her *God-given* nature. These are things I knew I could trust.

I could also trust my ability to prepare Mandy, so we sat down and had a long talk. We discussed what could go wrong at a sleepover—everything from fighting friends to smoking older brothers to throwing up. We set a certain time that I would call under some pretense (I think it was to ask if she'd packed her allergy medicine) just to check in. Then we created a reason for her to call home if she felt uncomfortable. We decided that she could tell the mom she had a stomachache and call me to come get her under any circumstances. That way, if it was something questionable that would be hard to tell the parent—such as an inappropriate movie, weird behavior, or a pet that scared her—she'd have an easy out. And I promised to come get her *no matter what time it was.*

I cannot tell you I was calm when I dropped her off. I was nervous. Even though I'd called a family that knew the household in question better than I did (they were sending their daughter too, so that helped things a bit), I said any number of prayers as I walked back to the car after dropping her off. I realized, though, that I had to trust the strength of the wire my daughter and I had strung. Trust her judgment. Trust the prayers I had said for her wisdom and protection. Trust that God had the ability to work in the situation no matter what occurred. Trust that there will always be scary but valuable times when I simply can't know everything to my comfort level.

What I had to trust here, what moms of ten-, eleven-, and twelve-year-olds wrestle with daily, is the uncomfortable knowledge that the challenges our children face are now becoming *their* challenges. As in "not *our* challenges." Somewhere underneath all that caution was the bone-deep knowledge that Mandy's handling of this situation was *Mandy's* bridge to cross. Sure, I firmly believe there are times when our Mommy Alert Systems go off and we have to pull our kids back from a situation no matter how much they protest. But I think all mothers come preloaded with the innate knowledge to know what those times are. And I knew this was not one of them.

I believe parenting is the continual process of wisely chosen releases. I believe the good fear comes in recognizing that we must let go in increasingly bigger issues so that when our kids face the really whopping issues they've got some experience under their belts. So rather than choose fear, I believe we must teach ourselves to gain a trembling trust in God's promise of protection and in our children. We need to train ourselves to stand firm, recognizing that most growth occurs in situations of risk.

Meanwhile, back at the sleepover ...

It certainly wasn't the greatest sleepover of all time, but it was a memorable one. And not for the reasons you'd expect. It was an important milestone.

Mandy called after about three hours and came home. We learned several

> I believe parenting is the continual process of wisely chosen releases.

things that night. Most practically, we learned that Mandy simply cannot tolerate being in a home with cigarette smoke—something I hadn't even thought to consider. Something, by the way, that Mandy figured out before I did. But there were other factors in her wise decision. Some things at that house simply made her uncomfortable. She wisely chose to listen to her gut when it said, "not a good situation." This, as far as I'm concerned, is a crucial life skill she'll need when those aforementioned whopping issues are staring her in the face. A skill she can only learn in tension-soaked circumstances. A trust we both needed to develop.

As a parent, I learned that if we give Mandy the tools to make good decisions, she does, in fact, make good decisions. My trust in Mandy strengthened that night. My trust grew in the prayer that protected her and empowered her wisdom.

Just as important is the fact that Mandy learned *I trust her*. She grew from the tension of that situation and her own ability to make a wise choice. She learned how strong her wire was and that it could get her across. We both added to what Dr. Cartmell calls "our personal bank of evidence" that changed our perceptions and reduced our fears.

> The plain, hard truth is that I don't think we could have learned this any other way. We had to have the tension to win the trust — trust that will become the best antidote for the next bout of tension.

The plain, hard truth is that I don't think we could have learned this any other way. We had to have the tension to win the trust—trust that will become the best antidote for the next bout of tension. One that most likely will be bigger than a sleepover.

I was intrigued to discover that the Chinese character for *crisis* is a combination of the characters for *danger* and *opportunity*. Hmm. Makes you think, doesn't it, that we all too often jump to the danger and forget the opportunity.

Next time you find yourself facing your child's risk, see if you can string your own wire with him or her across the impossible-looking gap. Never forget that the wire can be a very worthwhile place. Make sure, before you squelch that risky situation, that you aren't missing an essential opportunity to build trust.

In you.

In your child.

In the God who loves you both.

Fear-Facing Questions

Where in your parenting do you feel the tension between threat versus growth opportunity? What do you do in those situations? Are you comfortable with how you handle them? Or are there things you wish you could change?

Fear Fighter

Before you back away from a threatening situation, identify the opposing forces building your tension. Can that tension string you a wire bridge? Have the conversations; make the plans (and the contingency plans) that will enable you to trust. It might keep you from shying away from uncomfortable but important growth opportunities.

Faith-Finding Verse

Who among you fears the Lord and obeys the word of his servant? Let him who walks in the dark, who has no light, trust in the name of the Lord and rely on his God.

Isaiah 50:10

Challenge 2:
We Fear When It Feels Like We're Trapped

Sometimes the Only Way Over the Bridge
Is Over the Bridge

It's easy to stay calm when a workable solution presents itself. In parenting, though, workable solutions don't pop up every day. We often find ourselves tensely choosing between the lesser of two evils, making decisions with incomplete information, and simply not knowing what's best. We're stumped. When it's not clear where to turn, that's when our pulses soar.

Then there are those times when choosing doesn't even enter the picture. When something or someone leaves us with no choices at all, that's a surefire recipe for fear.

This year, while visiting my brother in Washington D.C., we were given the opportunity to travel over an engineering marvel called the William Preston Lane Jr. Memorial Bridge. Locals call it the Bay Bridge. Granted, it's no Golden Gate, but it is a fantastic, long, graceful, sweeping structure that travels 4.1 miles over some spectacular scenery. We went out of our way, paying the toll to boot, just to go over it. I was excited; the kids were excited. As it came into view, it was well worth the effort.

As we started up the small incline, though, traffic backed up. My brother, Joe, remarked that there might be someone stalled up ahead. Imagine my surprise when I discovered Joe didn't mean a stalled car—he meant a stalled *person*. Someone so overcome by the height and width of the bridge—and the massive expanse of water it traversed—that fear paralyzed the person, making him or her too afraid to drive over the bridge, even though hundreds of cars were doing it around his or her car.

As we discussed this human phenomenon, we saw her. I knew it just by looking at her. I could have picked her out even if it weren't obvious by her car's location. A young mom in a compact car, biting her lip, white-knuckled grip on the steering wheel. Knowing she had to get across but frozen and nearly flinching with every blink of her hazard lights. My heart went out to her—her perfectly human fear now amplified by the hundreds of staring motorists forced to work their way around her.

Did she know it would be scary? Or did it just leap out at her once she rounded the bend and the bridge came into view? If she knew the bridge would scare her, what was so important on the other side? My curious brain began to weave scenarios. A relative? A medical expert? Home? You could see it in her face: the need to get across combined with the panic-born inability to move into action.

My brother told me that this type of thing is quite common on this bridge. The nice folks at the Maryland Transportation Authority told me this happens over a dozen times a day. Anyone out there who freaks at bridges, rest in the knowledge that you seem to have lots of company.

I was amazed. I would never have even dreamed of being afraid. It wouldn't even occur to me that you *could* fear a bridge. But you can bet it was as real as real could be to that mom.

Why so much fear? Why is this bridge so scary?

Well, for one thing, it looks *narrow*. You've got some concrete pavement surrounding you on the westbound side, but on the eastbound side you're practically looking out your window into the bay through a few entirely-too-narrow-looking guardrails. Trying to look at the bridge through that mother's eyes, I could sense a trickle of fear finding its way up my spine. Sure, I knew the likelihood of my brother suddenly swerving off the lane, somehow managing to jump the specially built guardrail and plunging us into the bay, was slim to none. If it wasn't impossible, it certainly was improbable. Highly unlikely, especially when you consider that in the space of time we spent on the bridge I'd estimate that two hundred to three hundred cars made it successfully from one side to the other. Something like 100,000 cars drive over that bridge every day—most drivers without giving it a second thought.

Truth is, the Bay Bridge is more than strong enough, more than wide enough. It's endured hurricanes, huge trucks, and storms of every size and shape. One little car surely was in no real danger. But when we are channeled into those lanes, blocked in by dividers and barricades (even though their *sole purpose* is our safety), we feel trapped even with an open lane right in front of us. Once you go through the tollbooth on this bridge, you're committed. Turning around simply isn't an option. And stopping, as we all found out, has unpleasant consequences. The only way over was *over.*

What we, as parents, can draw from this experience is that *perception is everything.* In a situation in which the only way over is over, it's important to remember what Dr. Cartmell says about fear: It is a function of perception. *Narrow* is a perception. What's narrow to me looks expansive to a mouse. I did not see the bridge as narrow but as wide enough. That's why I wasn't afraid. That mother, however, saw it as narrow, and her fear followed that perception.

As we inched our way through the bridge traffic jam the woman had caused, I asked my brother what they do when this sort of thing happens. I fully expected the answer to be that the woman gets out and flags down some sort of state trooper who pulls her car over to the side, etc.—until I remembered that *there is no side on which to pull over.* No option of turning around. They don't let you back down the onramp.

My brother told me the bridge authority sends out a worker who *drives you across.* You can even request this in advance, I understand.

The solution struck me not only as obvious but as a wise metaphor as well. Like most deep truths, it's potent and simple: When you can't drive, get out of the driver's seat and let someone else drive.

What feels fearful to us may not to someone else. Someone like a spouse, a friend, or even our own child. It is wise to harness the power of someone else's less fearful perception.

Why? Because what may feel like a trap to me may actually be an opportunity. I won't see that opportunity, though, if I can't call on someone else to help change my perception.

> *What feels fearful to us may not to someone else. Someone like a spouse, a friend, or even our own child. It is wise to harness the power of someone else's less fearful perception.*

I learned this truth during a very difficult writing challenge. This particular project needed to satisfy two seemingly conflicting goals. I felt like the living personification of those subset diagrams from elementary school. You know, the ones where there is one blue circle and one yellow circle, and they overlap just the tiniest bit to show us that when you put blue and yellow together you get green. Well, I wasn't seeing a whole lot of green to work with. The blue and yellows of this project were warring with each other—in my very stomach, it felt like—leaving me only a tiny shred of green. And in this instance, the green was a very, very important issue for me. It was a very scary place to be.

If you have no plans to pen the great American novel, why bother telling you this? Because as I whined on the phone to a friend about not being able to pull this off, my friend said a very important, powerful thing. "Allie," she said, "it's narrow, but it's *wide enough.*"

"They're only giving me an inch of room!" I moaned.

"So take that inch and *live* in it," she replied.

Suddenly I realized that my goal, my calling in this particular project, was to live in that inch. To squeeze every blessed micron out of that inch. To stretch it in every direction. To *thrive* in that tiny space given me. I began to think of myself not as trapped but as supremely focused. I began to realize that the lesson for me in this project, the gifts I brought to it, were all about living in that inch. God had called me to this project *because* of that inch.

My writing friend was my driver over the bridge. She came into that situation beside me and did my "driving"—reframing the situation into something I could handle. Allowing me to see the opportunity hiding behind the threat.

Perhaps you are facing a mothering challenge that feels like that inch. Perhaps you are coping with a special needs child or facing the uncomfortable prospect of uprooting your family to a new location. You might be struggling with heavy-duty rebellion in a child that is going to require some truly drastic measures. Maybe you might have to go back to work part time when you'd rather be home full time. Maybe your checkbook is forcing you to send your kids to a public school when you'd rather they attend that nice private school up the street. Let's face it: for moms, the inches are everywhere.

When you fear you're being robbed of your choices and you're afraid for what may happen, remember this: that writing "inch" is one of the things I am most proud of in my career. It was also one of the hardest things I've ever done. I learned a great deal milking that inch for all it was worth. It was narrow—gut-wrenchingly so—*but it was wide enough.*

Do you feel like you've been sucked into an "inch"? (Doesn't it always feel like you've been "sucked into" situations like that? It never feels like we walked into them of our own accord.) If so, what's a girl to do?

Remember that *narrow* for you is often *wide enough* for someone else. It's the perception thing again. Find that someone else and let him or her help you. My high-wire teachers walk across the wire calmly, casually, and easily. That's why they can help me. A tollway worker could calmly and safely get that mother and her family across the bridge. My writing friend was the perfect "someone else" for that particular writing dilemma. I called her because I knew she was the one with whom to talk through this particular problem.

> Narrow for you is often wide enough for someone else. Find that someone else and let him or her help you.

Which means that I also knew who *not* to call. Moms, if you're shaking in your shoes, think carefully about whom you call. I'm guessing you know exactly what I mean. Sometimes, in a high-tension situation, your best friend is *not* who you should be calling. Everyone's got friends of both types: those who are the voice of calm and reason when the chips are down and those who can stir a tempest in a teapot in ten seconds flat. That's not to say that either is the better friend. It's simply realizing who is the wisest ally to get in the car with you so you can get over that bridge. On the Bay Bridge, that frightened mom needed someone who knew the situation, lacked the fear, and had the experience. In that case, the tollway worker— someone whose working life is spent on or near that bridge—was the perfect rescue party.

Not every friend makes a good rescue party, and that's perfectly okay. Those quick-to-panic friends have other gifts. They are often the ones with the souls of poets—they're the ones you want when you're sad or need to celebrate. But when fear backs you into a corner, you need your friend with the soul of a warrior.

This is exactly why every mom should cultivate a few friends who have older children. Why Hearts at Home and groups like it can make such a difference in the life of a mother. We need to spend time with moms who have the unique perception earned only through experience. Women who can say with complete certainty that swallowing a nickel will not, in fact, kill your five-year-old. Mothers who can recall the sleepless anxiety of your seven-year-old's first sleepover—and advise you to simply plan on getting up to fetch him or her at 12:30 a.m. Women who can tell you that, although they were convinced it would happen, they *never did* actually drop their newborn.

> *We need to spend time with moms who have the unique perception earned only through experience. Women who can say with complete certainty that swallowing a nickel will not, in fact, kill your five-year-old.*

God cares about who is in your driver's seat. Your Creator knows your limitations and your deepest needs. He knows the person who will make the best rescue party for what you're facing. Ask him.

Ask him to send you friends and mentors. Before you pick up the phone, shout an SOS heavenward and ask him whom to call.

Even when things don't require a drastic SOS call, moving over and letting someone else drive works in many parenting scenarios. Don't be afraid to admit that there are times when someone else needs to parent. When Mandy has to do something she's not thrilled about at the dentist, my husband takes her. Why? Because Jeff doesn't fear the dentist and I do. What's the point of my transferring my anxiety to her in an already anxious situation when she could have a perfectly calm dad by her side?

When fear traps you and there's only one way to turn, turn up toward your heavenly Father. Then make sure you turn to a friend. Choose a rescue party who can help you realize the fear may only be your perception. Let your friend "drive you over the bridge." You may discover, like I did, that your trap is actually an opportunity in disguise. Because often, the other side is really worth reaching.

Fear-Facing Questions

Where are your "inches" in parenting? Examine them to see where they are "wide enough" given your gifts and abilities.

Fear Fighter

Get yourself a pool of "drivers." Go through your list of friends and pick two or three to serve as the best rescue parties. Recognize the ones who don't make good rescuers, and know that they bring other gifts to your friendship. Make sure you have the answer to the popular query: "Who ya gonna call?"

Faith-Finding Verse

Peace I leave with you; my peace I give you. I do not give to you as the world gives. Do not let your hearts be troubled and do not be afraid.

John 14:27

Challenge 3:
We Fear When We Think We'll Fail

*Have You Considered That You May
Not Actually Fall on Your Face If You Try?*

"What if. . .?"

"If only. . ."

These have been called the most tragic words in the English language.

They are also part of every mother's life. Part of every woman's life. We'll all be faced with challenges so daunting they make our knees buckle.

Ever had one of those children who are late walkers? Not because they can't, but because they won't do it until they're sure they can pull it off without falling?

I had one. I was one. In many ways, I still am.

"I won't do it if I stand a good chance of failing." I think those ought to be considered the most tragic words in the English language. God has been rather insistent about teaching me this. The book you are holding is no exception, for it has been pushing me far out of my comfort zone from the day I started writing it. If you only knew how much chocolate, coffee, sweat, and tears put these words on the page . . . well, you'd hug me if we ever met (please do!).

About half way through the writing of this book, a decision was made to push up the production schedule— hugely. Everyone agreed it was a good idea, but I was the one who had to say "yes" knowing it would turn my life inside out for a stretch of time. God had already been at work in my heart, growing a sense of urgency about the need for this book in our nerve-racking times. Still, a big piece of me wasn't convinced I could pull it off.

Our whole family deliberated over the course of a weekend, because the decision to speed up this book would affect everyone. It was my daughter, however, who clinched the decision for me. We were riding in the car, talking about the decision, and she asked me if I really, really thought God wanted me to write the book this quickly.

"Yes," I answered, "I really do. But I'm worried about all the other stuff that has to fall into place to make it happen." The good, rational, prepared parental school of thinking. *Don't want to overextend myself. Setting limits is good. Boundaries are wise.*

Mandy stared at me. "But if God wants you to do it, can't you trust that he'll make all the other stuff fall into place like you need?"

Gulp.

If you've never had the amazing experience of God speaking to you through your children, trust me, it's coming. Mandy could see what I couldn't. It wasn't the workload sending my pulse into the sky, it was the fact that I didn't trust God to make it work, even if I was sure it was his will. And I *was* sure. I was just scared.

> If you've never had the amazing experience of God speaking to you through your children, trust me, it's coming.

Amazing. The exact point of my fear was nailed right on the head by an eleven-year-old girl with more accurate perception than her forty-year-old mother. Ain't parenthood grand?

In our parenting—as well as in our lives—God often calls us beyond our comfort zones to the places where we stand a very good chance of falling on our faces. To the high wires. To the places where, if he doesn't show up and be God, we're sunk.

But that's the point, isn't it? God *does* show up. Sometimes our fears come from forgetting his sovereignty. The

Bible—Psalm 139 in particular—is filled with wonderful, comforting references to how well God knows us. He created us. He knows us better than we know ourselves. He knows our gifts, our failings, and our needs even before we know them. He knows our future—both where we'll be and what we'll be—and desires only good things for us. And the most difficult to swallow but perhaps the most trust-engendering fact of all is that he knows that "good things" don't always mean "comfortable things" or "easy things."

In perhaps one of Isaiah's more famous verses, God tells us, "Fear not, for I have redeemed you; I have summoned you by name; and you are mine. When you pass through the waters, I will be with you; and when you pass through the rivers, they will not sweep over you. When you walk through the fire, you will not be burned" (Isa. 43:1–2). Notice the absence of nice, safe traveling here. Fire, water, burning, sweeping over—these are the stuff of disaster movies, not garden paths.

Our parenthood is filled with fire and raging water. Our children may possess personalities or even disabilities that feel far beyond our capacities. Spouses do die. Children can make disastrous choices. Illness happens. We can be relocated far away from those we love. Life happens.

All too often we have overwhelming evidence of our potential to fail. We must not forget what God can do in those kinds of places. Ours is the same God who calmed the storm and allowed Peter to walk on water, who raised Lazarus from the dead, and who fed thousands from a single lunch basket. Learn to lean on the mighty power of God to get us across those fearful bridges. Our faith in him becomes the strongest wire of all.

Nurture your faith and you will find that courage comes in the wake. I am a firm believer in asking God for what I term "blunt guidance." No subtlety here, please. I'd like a burning bush with Charleton Heston's voice coming out of it, thank you. Now, I can't say Mr. Heston has appeared within a flaming hedge anywhere in my backyard, but I can tell you that God has kindly answered my request to be painfully obvious many times. As you heard, he's even used my daughter as an unexpectedly accurate mouthpiece. Notice I didn't say God's guidance was easy—just blunt and unmistakable.

As I plunged into the tightened deadline to get this book done, God strengthened my faith and my trust one day at a time. Each morning I listed for the Lord my needs for that day. Everything from "keep the kids from getting sick" to "give me time to exercise." Or, "can someone please ask CJ over for a playdate?" to "I don't know how to fix this paragraph," to "send me this resource or an idea for this chapter." I wrote them down like a to-do list, complete with a check-off box after each need. Every morning, before starting that day's list, I'd go back to the day before and check off all the things God provided. I'm here to tell you there are very few unchecked boxes. Big things, small things, I'm growing my faith in God's ability to answer prayer—to do what Mandy already knew he'd do.

> I am a firm believer in asking God for what I term "blunt guidance." No subtlety here, please. I'd like a burning bush with Charleton Heston's voice coming out of it, thank you.

When I built my trust in God to take care of my needs, my faith grew. It is still growing. Sure, I've panicked. I've backslid. But I know daily, right this very minute, that God is building my faith to fight my fear.

Thankfully, the Bible—especially the book of Psalms—is chock full of verses to remind us of this. "God is our refuge and strength, an ever-present help in trouble. Therefore we will not fear, though the earth give way and the mountains fall into the heart of the sea" (Ps. 46:1–2). "If you make the

Most High your dwelling—even the LORD, who is my refuge—then no harm will befall you, no disaster will come near your tent. For he will command his angels concerning you to guard you in all your ways" (Ps. 91:9–11).

There have been times when my inability to control a situation or my ultimate fear and frustration over a problem has finally forced me to throw it at God's feet in desperation. And I do mean throw. I've yelled and stamped my feet. I've cried and wailed. I've actually thrown writing manuscripts across the room. I've scrawled "It's God's Problem" across papers, on bathroom mirrors, and across parenting books, report cards, and notes from teachers. I'd have scrawled it across a box of training pants if it would have stuck—my son was *so* averse to potty training.

Some people use the concept of God boxes or prayer bowls in which you write down your problem, stick it inside, and then consider it officially out of your hands. I've yet to be able to actually let it go when I've tried it—God's not done with me yet. But I will tell you that I have received answers to those kinds of prayers despite my inability to divinely delegate. Because guess what? It *is* God's problem. He's a trustworthy God who has a much different view than you do. No matter what you fear—everything from labor to overdue bills to even death—God is bigger than it.

Parenting is full of the potential for spectacular failures. But it's also full of the potential for spectacular growth. On my car radio this morning I heard a pastor say that while fear is the anticipation of bad things coming our way, faith is the anticipation of good things coming our way.

It is faith—it will always be faith—that makes the difference.

Fear-Facing Questions

Where do you need to nurture your faith in order to find courage? Where do you need to see more evidence of God's sovereignty in your life? How can you find ways to see it?

Fear Fighter

Gain access to God's "blunt guidance" right now. Take a moment and ask God to be painfully obvious in sending you the help you need. Write your request down, if you can, and use a God box if it helps. As you submit it to either your journal or your box, say to yourself (out loud), "It's *God's* problem now!" Whatever form you choose, make sure you can also record the answer to your prayer when it comes.

Faith-Finding Verse

Fear not, for I have redeemed you; I have summoned you by name; you are mine. When you pass through the waters, I will be with you; and when you pass through the rivers, they will not sweep over you. When you walk through the fire, you will not be burned.

Isaiah 43:1–3

Trustworthy Cable Is No Accident

It is hard—very hard—to stand back and let our children take risks. Even though risk is quite often the best path to growth, it's not going to feel comfy. But if we can arm ourselves to live with the tension, then we are better able to let the risk spur the growth it can produce.

Living with tension is not everyone's first choice. Comfort and security feel a whole lot better. Often, when the only path to growth leads over risky, rocky ground, we feel trapped. We let that single path be a source of fear rather than focus. The *just do its* of life are hardly ever fun. But again, we'll cope far better if we recognize this isn't a comfortable situation, that fear is going to be part of the picture, and then take the path we need to take.

There's one more thing about this wire we're walking. No one gets it on their first try. I had half a dozen lessons before I made it ten feet across. I failed a lot. But somewhere deep inside I knew I had the capacity to pull it off. Parenting often feels the same way. So many times it feels like it ought to be much easier. It ought to come much more naturally. We wonder if we can pull it off at all. Here is the place where trust and encouragement enter the picture. God himself placed these children into our keeping. He knows our faults and abilities even better than we know them ourselves. If he believes we can pull it off, then perhaps he can help us to believe the same.

The aerialists I've talked to both trust and mistrust their wire. The wire's rigging is checked and rechecked a dozen times, and not by just anybody. When the circus comes to town, local people are hired just for the weekend to help with numerous tasks. Important things, however, are only done by a very select group of stagehands—or in many cases by the artists themselves. It makes sense. If you're going to risk your life up there, you want to be able to trust the guy who rigged your line.

Our rigging as parents is no different. The good news here is that the guy who rigged *your* line is none other than THE GUY. God. I like to remind myself that God chose my children to come into my keeping. The particular combination of Mandy and Mom—aggravating or wonderful as it can be—is a blend uniquely designed for the two of us. God chose Mandy and CJ to be my children.

Some days it feels like we will never get from one platform to the other. We'll never see our kids master the skills and growth of childhood. The path looks too hard to take, too devoid of pleasant options, too beyond our abilities. When such feelings well up in you, try to think what you'd feel if you were looking at a high wire. Sure it looks scary and impossible, but people cross high wires. It is possible. I've got the snapshots to prove it.

The specialized combination of your motherhood—the blend of souls in your family—is the purposeful design of the Lord Almighty.

Who never makes mistakes.

Not ever.

Chapter 4

THE ALTITUDE

"I'm afraid my kids will look at me one day and feel that I failed them, and they won't be proud to call me their mom."

"My biggest fear is not being able to protect my children from harm, that someone will hurt them and I won't be able to prevent it."

"I fear I'll never feel in control ever again."

"I always fear that I'm missing something—some crucial life skill or school subject or character trait that I'm not teaching my child—and that he will be irreparably damaged because of that omission. I somehow feel as if there's a syllabus for life and I haven't got a copy."

We're Too High Up, Aren't We?

No matter how much you trust the strength of your wire, there's no getting around the fact that a high wire is just that—high. Very high. Standard high-wire height is forty feet off the ground (four stories, in case you were wondering). The bottom line—and this is part of the attraction—is that *danger is present*. Anyone walking that wire can fall. Even if you have a net under you, things can happen. Any aerialist will tell you people have been severely injured doing this sort of thing. People have died.

While I know of no actual fatalities, raising children often does feel just as death-defying. Parenting seems to have such a long, long way to fall. We parent up here at a dangerous altitude. It feels as if one wrong parenting choice can leave your kids in therapy, injured, or dead.

That feeling didn't form in a vacuum—there's a kernel of truth there. We know our parental influence can be wielded for good or ill. We don't even need personal life experience; the newspapers and television are filled with stories of adults gone wrong who cite bad parenting—or no parenting—as the seed of their destruction.

The pressure's on. Will we be the kind of parents who produce happy, successful adults? Or do we blow it and sign our kids up for a lifetime of therapy and dysfunction?

Everyone wants the answer to that question. We buy buckets of baby books because we want someone to assure us we're doing things right. Or we hope they will help us catch a mistake before the consequences become too dear. I'm always fearful of missing that little comment, that offhand remark that will let me know something's wrong with my children. I worry that I'll miss that first vital symptom that would have clued me into oncoming cancer or diabetes or depression . . . or worse. I fear that somehow my children will be falling into terrible emotional or physical danger and I won't see it. The older they get, the more powerful that fear becomes because they become so blasted uncommunicative in their teen years, and one tiny shred of dialogue may be all you get.

In parenting, things could go wrong at any moment. Any misstep could spell our doom. We're not entirely wrong when we convince ourselves that *everything* matters, that every ounce of nutrition, every minute of quality parenting, every teachable moment missed is irreplaceable.

Life *is* scary. There's no getting around it—parenting has high stakes. We are attempting a dangerous feat up here on the maternal high wire. Parenting surely isn't for wimps; this stress could crumple anyone. How, then, are we to cope? For starters, we need to remember that altitude has two sides. Yes, it increases the danger, but you have to remember that it also *increases visibility*.

> We're not entirely wrong when we convince ourselves that everything matters, that every ounce of nutrition, every minute of quality parenting, every teachable moment missed is irreplaceable.

Think about being in a maze. You're running around bumping into dead ends left and right, building tension with each wrong turn. What if you found a tower in one of those corners? Something you could climb up that would place your viewpoint above the walls so you could plot the right course to your exit? Sure you could slip and fall off the tower and hurt yourself, but there'd be no mistaking that climbing the tower would give you the advantage of vision.

The vision of altitude comes at the price of danger. My high-wire teachers have taught me the importance of respecting danger. That's *not* the same thing as avoiding danger. When you get right down to it, it's rarely the danger that's dangerous as much as it is *failing to acknowledge it.*

We're going to spend this section acknowledging parenthood's dangers. They are there. To pretend they're not is to buy into the lie of denial. By acknowledging the danger, we allow ourselves to choose the wisest path to our goal. We'll look at why high wires call for the very best equipment and why getting up out of your worry and doing something is often the wisest path of all. We'll call upon the power of memory to encourage and reassure us that the height is not as foreign as it seems.

Hey, we're up here. Wouldn't it be a shame to miss the view?

Challenge 1:
We Fear Our Children Coming to Harm
The Ferocious Child-Eating Monkey Bars of Death

Having kids is like receiving your own personal invitation to visit the emergency room. You invite danger in the door when you become a parent.

Danger, though, is a tricky concept. Lots of times it's hard to know what danger really is. There are many, many families on earth who face real dangers every single day. Societies have raised children in the midst of mortar fire. Countries have been locked in civil wars that have family members killing family members for decades. Babies have been born amid acts of ethnic cleansing. Then there's drought or rampant disease. Folks, that's real danger.

My head understands the concept of real danger. My heart, though, loves to see danger in places it doesn't really exist. Places much closer to home. To tell the truth, it's the monkey bars that truly do me in. Now monkey bars are not a real danger. I can *say* that, but you can bet your HMO my heart doesn't believe it for a second. Mandy often chides me for my playground posture: standing on the sidelines, hands over my mouth, a look of certain doom on my face. Lots of sucking in my breath and such. Never mind the smart bombs, this mom lives in fear of the monkey bars.

It's funny, though, because I don't have a *single memory* of hurting myself on the playground. Still, playgrounds make me nervous. All that equipment just looks to me like a trip to the emergency room. Even though in a dozen years of parenting my fears have never (at least so far) been realized.

Another mother, no doubt in response to my state of nerves, once said the most amazing thing to me about her children on the playground. Our children were playing together, and she was calmly holding a conversation while I kept halting to gasp anew at some act of daring by my child. As she raised that eyebrow at me—you know, the one that comes with the "get over it" expression—she said, "Let 'em climb whatever they want."

I feel compelled to point out here, in my defense, that my son was three at the time. Three, folks—that's barely out of diapers. Granted, we were at the tot lot, but three is still very, very small.

> *This mom just looked at me and calmly said, "So she breaks an arm." So she breaks an arm? Moms aren't supposed to say those kinds of things, are they?*

At this point in the conversation I am sure one of her daughters slipped a good four feet off some playground equipment, catching herself *j-u-s-t* before her head crashed onto the beam below. Mrs. Calm Mom didn't even flinch—though I was flinching enough for the both of us.

"She almost fell!" I gasped.

"Yes," said the mom, as if this were the most obvious thing in the world.

"Aren't you afraid she'll get hurt?"

"She *will* get hurt sometimes."

My eyes popped out at this point. Like some sort of Mom-cliche we all groaned about in junior high, I said, "What if she breaks an arm or something?" Can you just hear, "It's all funny until somebody gets hurt!" or, "You could poke an eye out with that thing!" ringing in your ears?

This mom just looked at me and calmly said, "So she breaks an arm." *So she breaks an arm?* Moms aren't supposed to say those kinds of things, are they?

I couldn't believe how casually she handled this. But Mrs. Calm Mom recognized, far more clearly than I did, that life isn't always safe. Kids get hurt, and it isn't the end of the world. Mrs. Calm Mom knew that if you have lots and lots and lots of rambunctious fun, sooner or later the odds will catch up to you and you'll suffer an injury. Then you'll see a doctor. Then you'll heal and go back to have lots and lots more fun. She recognized the altitude and had made peace with it. I sure hadn't.

It was hours later that the truth of what Mrs. Calm Mom said struck me. Really, what's the worst that can happen at the tot lot? Broken bones, stitches, etc. are about the worst-case scenario in there. With astonishment I mentally inventoried my lifetime supply of broken bones. Both legs (not at the same time), one arm, two toes, and a thumb. Nearly every major limb by the time I was thirty-five.

Am I fine?

Yes.

In the grand scope of things I've considered damaging in my life, do I count broken bones among them?

No.

Do I know kids who have broken arms on the playground?

Yes. I even have a friend who suffered a significant, life-threatening head injury on the playground as a child (and even *she's* calmer beside the monkey bars than I).

Are they fine?

Yes.

The answer astounded me. Yes, they're fine. In the real, truest sense of danger, there was no significant danger here. Was I acting like there was? You bet. So much so that even my own kids were picking up on it.

Therapist Jenny Gresko remembers an annual childhood sledding extravaganza landing her in the ER more than once. She pointed out, "Getting hurt has now become a terrible thing. It didn't used to be that way. Going to the emergency room for a broken bone or a sprain used to be a part of childhood. It is *we* who have now turned it into a crisis."

When did we make childhood so scary? Was it the world, or just us? I believe parenthood became a house of horrors when we stopped fearing what's worth fearing and began fearing *everything*. It's a natural progression—if we've convinced ourselves that everything matters, then everything can harm you.

Think back to your early days as a parent. Remember your baby's first high fever? It's one of the experiences that feel life-and-death for new parents. If your experience was like mine, it was about 3:30 a.m., and all your house lights were on because you and your husband were wide awake scanning *Dr. Spock's Baby and Child Care* and every other book you could get your hands on, wondering if you should page your doctor or visit the emergency room. Your sleep-deprived brain was concocting all sorts of life-threatening viruses, seizures, and deadly diseases, each one ready to do in your little one at a moment's notice. Every episode of *ER* you'd ever seen, every medical horror story you'd heard, every outcome from flesh-eating bacteria to lifelong disability was playing in your head as you wrestled one more time with the child-safety cap on the baby Tylenol. You stared at your husband wondering, "What do we do?" You felt as though her tiny new life was at stake, and the entire burden was falling on your shoulders.

The truth of the matter, though, is that with very few exceptions your fever-ridden child was *not* in danger. For those first few hours, the simple things you already knew to do were, in fact, what you ought to do. Liquids, Tylenol, cool cloths, soothing voices. Yet those nights felt desperate.

How easily we can convince ourselves that their little lives hang in the balance of whether or not we catch each and every symptom. How easily a troublesome cough becomes bronchitis or pneumonia in our novice-parent brains. Suddenly we're practically dissecting our babies, peering into every nook and cranny, scrutinizing every inch of their skin. Oh how quickly a bump becomes a potential chicken-pock.

Now add some national anxiety to the mix, and it's easy to see how parenting has gotten really jumpy. I *feel* like parenting is much harder today than it was twenty years ago. During the summer of 2002, every mosquito bite in Chicago held the threat of West Nile Virus. In 2001 every letter with a missing return address posed a potential threat. We all feel as though this generation is living with more fear than the last. Snipers, national security alerts, countries brandishing nuclear weapons—it's enough to make you run for your Ben and Jerry's on a daily basis. No matter how many facts I throw at it, my brain still refuses to be convinced that we're not the most threatened generation in history—that someone hasn't raised our high wire a dozen feet higher than everyone else's.

But we're not. Make yourself say that out loud right now: "We're not." More fear doesn't automatically equal more danger. It only means more *fear*. The actual dangers to our immediate family are, for the most part, *perceived*.

> No matter how many facts I throw at it, my brain still refuses to be convinced that we're not the most threatened generation in history—that someone hasn't raised our high wire a dozen feet higher than everyone else's.

Families who have lived through the world wars or who've been in third world countries know actual danger. The February 24, 2003, *Newsweek* put it in hard fact: "Though America's current worries may seem unprecedented, the current situation has nothing on the 1918 flu epidemic or the Cuban missile crisis."

In the scramble to capture our overloaded concentration, the media has become downright predatory in its efforts to find and show something attention-grabbing. The one-in-a-million story now gets a showing in a million homes. According to the Harvard Center for Risk Analysis, the average American's risk for being shot by a sniper (something every Washington D.C. parent was concerned about in November 2002) is 1 in 517,000. Compare that with the odds of developing heart disease—1 in 4—and you get a little perspective.

It's important that we fear the things that *ought to be feared*. We should take a moment and identify the *real* dangers facing our children rather than spending so much energy reacting to what only *feels* dangerous. Your child has a 1 in 3,000,000 chance of dying in an airplane crash. But if your child takes up smoking, he or she has a 1 in 2 chance of dying from a smoking-related illness. Which do you think is more worthy of your attention?

We focus on the big, vague dangers because it's easier. Author Gavin deBecker nails it on the head, "We tend to give our full attention to risks that are beyond our control (plane crashes, nuclear-plant disasters) while ignoring those we feel in charge of (dying from smoking, poor diet, car accidents), even though the latter are far more likely to harm us."[6] To focus on the real dangers is to face up to our lack of control over some things.

Well all right then, what *should* hold our attention? As far as I can tell, the three most significant dangers to our kids are: (1) abduction and/or perpetrated violence of any sort, (2) abuse—by their use of substances or to them in terms of physical, emotional, or sexual abuse, and (3) what I'll term "corruption"—friends who are bad influences, choices that head them down the wrong road in life, etc. Each of these can wreck a life—or take a life. That list will raise your pulse just by reading it. Every parent's nightmare, right?

Look again at those three big dangers. While they have physical manifestations, their lasting damage is *to the soul*.

Therein lies the *real* danger facing our children. Not physical danger, but spiritual danger. We moms are so quick to think of body-danger, but it's the soul-danger that should hold our attention.

You'd think it would be uncomfortable to give such dangers so much attention. But like the Joker yelling into the night, "I have given a name to my pain, and that pain is Batman!" naming our real dangers becomes the defiant foothold that allows us to fear less and act more sensibly.

The answer seems to be a daily refocusing, a constant reminder of what's really worth the worry. Here's where the Bible's exhortation for us in Luke 12:4–5 to worry more about what can harm a soul than what can harm a body becomes my daily chant. It helps me in my daily struggle against my very human impulse to worry about things that don't merit my anxiety. It is my daily prayer to focus more on the broken spirit than the broken bone.

Sure, it's uncomfortable to focus my fears away from the plane crash on the TV news and onto the sticky social mire of middle-school popularity contests. It's hard to be more worried about whether she reads a Bible than whether she reads at her grade level. The plane crash and reading score are so much more finite, so much less intimate than the other issues.

I have found, however, that owning up to the real dangers facing my children grants me the perspective I need to not sweat the small stuff. And it helps me recognize that the lesson, "I can be seriously hurt and survive," may be the most powerful outcome of a broken arm.

> Recognize that the lesson, "I can be seriously hurt and survive," may be the most powerful outcome of a broken arm.

The easiest way to retrain the brain, I have found, is to play "Worst-Case Scenario." Having a high-octane imagination like mine plays well into this game, but I'm guessing nearly every mom can nudge her own imagination toward the extreme. Take whatever it is you fear and give your brain permission to spin the worst possible outcome. Take those monkey bars and imagine that broken arm. Make it a really bad break. Go ahead, have him lose a couple of fingers. Now take a good hard look. Can your son still be a successful adult? Can he still fall in love and get married and give you adorable grandchildren? Might the teasing he gets for having a disfigurement make him a stronger person and give his heart a wealth of compassion? Can he still love and serve God? Is he still capable of the things you care about most for his life? Do you know someone who's endured even more and come out stronger for it?

The answer to those questions—unless you possess a truly macabre bent—is most likely "yes." When you continue to force yourself down that extreme path, you will find that gradually it makes less and less sense to worry about skateboards and hot dog nitrates. The question of whether CJ will catch cold if he plays outside without a jacket holds less tension for me now. I am inching my way toward Mrs. Calm Mom.

I really want to be Mrs. Calm Mom. Don't you?

Fear-Facing Questions

What perceived dangers to your children worry you the most? Are they really things within your control? Which of Allie's "big three" dangers is most uncomfortable for you to contemplate? Why?

Fear Fighter

Take your favorite fear and play "Worst-Case Scenario." Is it really damaging? Does it really affect the things you want most for your child? Let the answers to those types of questions refocus your attention. Do it in writing if you need to, because sometimes seeing it in black and white makes it easier to recognize an extreme thought as unrealistic.

Faith-Finding Verse

I tell you, my friends, do not be afraid of those who kill the body and after that can do no more. But I will show you whom you should fear: Fear him who, after the killing of the body, has power to throw you into hell. Yes, I tell you, fear him. Are not five sparrows sold for two pennies? Yet not one of them is forgotten by God.

Luke 12:4–6

Challenge 2:
We Fear It's Out of Our Control

Why the Blue Power Ranger May
Have One Up on the Rest of Us

If you ask any aerialist, he or she will tell you that one of the best ways to cope with the dangers of altitude is to use the very best equipment. Training and equipment enable the high-wire walker to accomplish those seemingly impossible feats. Simply put, you fight real danger with strong equipment.

Our children are no different. I learned this lesson, though, in a most unexpected place. Two years ago I was looking for a nonteam sport to give my son some physical training. At that time, the Power Rangers ruled supreme in my house (and no, I wasn't thrilled about that, but any mother of a five-year-old boy will tell you some battles aren't worth having). When I gave CJ the choice between gymnastics and karate, he chose the latter, especially when he learned our local instructor knew, *actually knew*, the Blue Ranger. Wow!

Sensei Steve, as he is called, is one part karate teacher, two parts stand-up comic. CJ loves him and has tons of fun in class. But Steve weaves some very potent safety issues into his classes. The more I watched, the more I realized this wasn't just about physical fitness but also equipping CJ with skills and tools to protect himself in a bad situation.

I had framed karate in a Jackie Chan kung-fu movie bracket in my mind. When Steve taught the kids what to do if a stranger grabs them, my brain woke up. Sure, we did the "stranger danger" thing like all good parents, but had I *equipped* my children? Not in the effective way Steve did. He taught my son to yell at someone approaching him, "Stop! Go Away!" He taught him to put his hands up in a defensive posture that made it clear to anyone that CJ did not want to be near this person. And, perhaps most chilling of all, he taught him to yell, "This is not my mom!" or, "This is not my dad!" if someone tried to drag him out of a public place.

Think about it—how many times have we seen a screaming child dragged from the mall and not given it a second thought, assuming it was a parent dealing with a tantrum? Yet what do moms across America list as one of their number one fears? Their child being abducted from a public place like a playground or a mall.

> I'm far better off worrying, "Does he know what to do if it happens?" than worrying, "Will it happen?"

I'm not advocating rushing out to your nearest martial arts studio and enrolling your kids. I think the answer will be different for each family, for each individual child. But the karate studio got me thinking about what's useful worry and what's useless worry. I'm far better off worrying, "Does he know what to do if it happens?" than worrying, "Will it happen?" There's a clever saying that applies to this shift in thinking: "Worrying about problems is like looking at bacteria through a microscope; it doesn't help them go away, it just makes them look bigger." Worrying about the real dangers without focusing that energy to equip your child to deal with it is like staring at those bacteria without ever reaching for the antibiotics.

I've discovered that if I can focus on *equipping my child* for a world with dangers in it, I'm tending to the part I *can* control in a problem that's largely *out* of my control. That equipping isn't just mental and physical; it's emotional and spiritual. When you look at our big three dangers, the corruption and abuse are largely relational—things that may start as small problems before they escalate into gigantic ones. Here is where the equipping is really about the relationship between our children and ourselves.

High wires are held up with support cables called *guy wires* or *cavalettis*—reinforced lines that pull the wire tight and keep it from swaying when pressure is applied. In the words of Philipe Petit, who stunned the world by walking a high wire strung between New York City's World Trade Center twin towers: "Their purpose is to reduce the vibrations on the wire. Because they create an area of steadiness, because they reduce the emptiness by constructing a three dimensional shape in the void, because they offer an additional object of visual focus, and because the wirewalker feels he can hold on to them in case of trouble, the places where cavaletti ropes connect with the cable always represent a safe haven. The wise rigger of high wires spaces his cavalettis prudently."[7]

Parents need to be just as prudent. Our relationship with our kids are their cavalettis. We're the ones who apply the force that hopefully keeps them from swaying when the pressure is applied. We're the ones who can hold up a worthy focus, who can create a safe haven. And pressure is coming in our children's lives, make no mistake about that.

I hope my child never has to face anything more dreadful than peer pressure—which any middle-school mom can tell you is a force to be reckoned with. As for the big stuff like the possibility of my daughter suffering some kind of abuse, I find it more productive to worry about the strength of our relationship than to worry if she'll encounter abuse. Sure, I do what I can, but I'll never be able to do enough to guarantee her protection. That can make me crazy or it can refocus my attention. The strength of our relationship will determine whether or not she comes to me with a concern about someone in her life. Our closeness might determine whether the "secret keeping" damage of any abuse will be weaker than her ability to trust me. And if we've nurtured her self-esteem and spiritual health, she won't be looking to fill up those voids with substances or unhealthy relationships.

The high-altitude truth is that I cannot always protect Amanda. The older she gets, the less I can protect her. If I spent my energy worrying about everyone with whom she comes in contact (some of whom are bound to be bad people—let's just face that right now), I'd scare myself into hysteria.

I am not in control of her world. But I am in control of her support system. So I'm going to worry about the stuff I *can* control. Like how much time we have alone together to just talk. What is she feeling about herself and her appearance, and how I am helping her to cope with that? Is she feeling respected by this family? Have I shown her I trust her and she can trust me? Am I showing an active interest in what she enjoys? Am I making an effort to sit through listening to one of her CDs and find out why she likes that kind of music?

Let's take another example. Lots of moms I know—myself most definitely included—fear that their children will make the wrong kind of friends. Whether it's preschool or college seems to matter very little. We've been told over and over about the power of peer pressure and how it can drag our little angels down. I usually picture it like Darth Vader—dark cloak, exuding power, heavy breathing—beckoning Luke Skywalker to "come over to the Dark side of the Force." I tend to have a rather cinematic imagination. It's extreme, I know, but I'll be willing to bet many of you have a similar picture in your heads.

Again, this feels like a problem largely out of my control. In truth, parts of it are. But there are many elements that are in my control. I can seek out people who have children older than mine to mentor me. People who can give me a heads-up on the tough spots and help me know what's worth worrying about and what will probably pass. I can look for and listen to those people who know my children and their strengths. Someone (i.e., a reasonably objective nonrelative) who can say, "That CJ, he's a compassionate child. He makes friends easily, cares about everyone's feelings." From a completely practical standpoint, I needed something fun and nurturing to do while he was in preschool so that I didn't sit at home and worry about whether or not he was running with scissors—or running with the wrong crowd. And every mom needs some friends who will calmly remind us that there isn't really a "wrong crowd" in preschool.

Even as we make our way through second grade now, I can take steps to get myself involved in CJ's social life. Take the time to see all the great friendships my son is making and how he's growing socially. I can make sure those lines of communication are wide open, listening to him tell me the stories of the fights and other sticky moments he's had. I can let him help me understand that he's learning how to navigate the choppy waters of interpersonal conflict. I can talk to him about which friends make him feel good about himself and why. About how to handle those people who don't make him feel good about himself. Help him, on his level, learn how to evaluate relationships and choose wisely.

You think your four-year-old is too young to be perceptive on this level? Ask any preschooler who's the class bully—he'll know right off, and he'll usually give you ten reasons why.

DeBecker, in his follow-up book *Protecting the Gift*, tells the astounding tale of the mom who taught her children to talk to strangers.[8] Talk to strangers! Moms shouldn't do that, should they? DeBecker thinks they should. And the reasons will amaze you.

Chances are that at some point in their lives your children will wind up lost and separated from you in a public place. We all fear it; many of us take careful steps to prevent it, but kids are sneaky beings and the world is full of nifty things that command their little attentions. Also, a world full of great big legs blocks any kind of view to get their bearings. Getting lost happens.

Does your child know what to do? Most of us would say "yes." Stay put, say a little prayer, find someone in a uniform and tell him or her you're lost. Stuff our moms told us.

Did you know, though, that while they're staying put, things can happen? I was surprised when deBecker praised a mother for teaching her child to seek out a stranger right away and get help. Why? Because, statistically speaking, your child is far safer with *someone he or she has picked out of a crowd* to ask for help than relying on *the person who seeks out the lost child.*

When I realized deBecker was right, it made me mighty nervous. Our children will always have good intentions when they seek someone out, but we can't be sure of someone's intentions in seeking out our child. Honestly, I'd never thought of it in those terms.

Here I was, doing the "stranger danger" thing, when the best equipment I could give my children was to teach them how to pick the best stranger to approach in a jam. The mother in deBecker's book began by teaching her children to ask a stranger for the time or for directions. She taught them to look for another mother with children—statistically the safest person to ask. She taught them—right in front of her watchful eye—to listen to that little voice inside that let them know this stranger was getting too close to their face or that stranger looked at them funny. It all made complete sense to me once deBecker explained it, but I would have called him nuts before he made his case. It's a solid argument for the value of good equipment.

The reason why deBecker's no-nonsense approach makes such sense comes from an important truth. An essential, albeit scary truth that, paradoxically, fights the fear. The truth is this: Children—good, well-cared-for children—*do* get hurt, abducted, and abused. Bad things happen to good kids, and good kids go bad. I know scores of excellent, loving parents who have sweated blood over their relationships with their children only to have those beloved children go very, very wrong. Horrible things happen. In those instances we must throw ourselves at the feet of a compassionate God and trust that someday we will know the sense of it all. It is better to look straight at such tragic circumstances and know that they are out of our control. Better to see the hard truth and choose to respond by controlling what we can and trusting God with the rest.

I cannot protect Amanda all day and night from those who would seek to harm her, but God can. And I can be relentless in commending her to his care. I can also continually nurture my trust that no damage will be done to her that God cannot use for good in her life.

God is trustworthy, but life is unsafe. We have the capacity to trust but not the certainty of guarantees. Our children will suffer things we, as parents, find unfair and cruel. Yet no matter how far they fall, no matter what happens to them, they are still under the protection of the Lord Almighty. For as the saying goes, "What does not kill us makes us stronger." Many who become great in this life often pay dearly for the privilege.

Think of all those great biblical heroes and look at their lives; they read like soap opera scripts. Job and his obliterated family members not to mention dozens of truly nasty illnesses. Joseph's imprisonment and abuse at the hands of brothers worthy of a Jerry Springer show. Moses' death-defying trek across the desert only to be demoted from Vice Pharaoh to smelly shepherd for a couple of dozen years. Can you *imagine* what their mothers went through? We forget that Moses' mom put her son out on the river without the luxury of reading Exodus. She didn't

> God is trustworthy, but life is unsafe. We have the capacity to trust but not the certainty of guarantees.

have the silver lining of hindsight that we have. I'll bet she grieved mightily over her son's misfortune after he left Egypt. She worried desperately that his future was lost. Possibly even gave him up for dead. God, of course, had other plans.

Can you believe God has other plans for you? For your child? No matter what happens? He does.

Fear-Facing Questions

What is the harm you most fear befalling your children? Do you just fear it, or have you researched how to fight it? You may be surprised to learn that the more you look that fear in the face and find the best equipment, the less you fear it. Discover what truly threatens your child and the best course of coping with it.

Fear Fighter

If you fear some particular bodily harm for your children, see if you can't locate someone who has survived that experience. Is there someone who has lived through cancer, abuse, or the death of a loved one? Talking with that person, learning how that experience may have shaped who he or she is, will help you. Identify the opposite of your fear, and make a list of three things you can do about it. Can you take a driver's course to decrease your fear of car crashes? Enroll yourself and your children in a self-defense class? Teach your children to talk to strangers wisely? Those tasks are far better places for your energy than fear or worry about something that is largely out of your control.

Faith-Finding Verse

For you did not receive a spirit that makes you a slave again to fear, but you received the Spirit of sonship. And by him we cry "Abba, Father."

Romans 8:15

Challenge 3:
We Fear We Can't Cope
You've Been There, You've Done That—Remember?

Motherhood seems to enjoy surprising us with new and unnerving situations. Whether you're holding your first newborn or taking a deep breath to hand over the car keys for the first time, life continually hands us situations that raise the fear we'll never be able to cope. In situations like these, it's important to remember that past coping can fuel confidence in your ability to cope with things that are yet to come. Once you've given birth, I bet when you are faced with some physical difficulty you said to yourself, "If I can get through labor, how hard can this be?"

In our first Lamaze class, our teacher did an interesting exercise. She laid a number line, one through ten, across the floor of our classroom. "One" meant no painkillers whatsoever; "ten" meant out-like-a-light sedated. She had the women go stand on the number they guessed might be their experience of labor. I stood on "five." Rather noncommittal of me, I understand, but I guessed I might need a little help with the really big contractions.

Then our teacher had the fathers-to-be stand on the numbers. Jeff walked straight to "one."

I was aghast. Okay, perhaps a tiny bit complimented at his assessment of my fortitude, but more worried. His beeline of confidence had me thinking I might hear a perky, "Come on, honey, you know you can do it!" when I was begging for my epidural.

Before you classify my husband as an insensitive oaf, you need to understand the reason for his choice. And you ought to know before I get any further that he was *absolutely correct*.

You see, Jeff had remembered something I hadn't: I was no stranger to prolonged pain. For most of my life I have suffered from debilitating migraines. My personal brand of migraine involved ten to twelve hours of intense pain, vomiting, and disorientation. Something for which, until ten years ago, I had no effective medicines to help me cope. As Jeff explained it, he didn't see how this was much different than a great big migraine—it even had a really wonderful prize (God willing) at the end of it. The only compensation I got for a migraine was about five pounds in water weight loss from getting so sick to my stomach (which, of course, I gained right back anyway). If I could endure migraine after migraine after migraine, chances were very good I could get through this one-time episode of labor.

And do you know what? I did. Before we had to opt for a C-section (Mandy was one stubborn little baby, let me tell you, but that's another story), I survived thirteen hours of labor including four hours of pushing with very little pain medicine. I believe this was partly because Jeff had held me up as a migraine survivor. He, in his nerve-racking choice of numbers, had reminded me of my capacity to endure pain. He strung that support wire of encouragement for me. It didn't belittle the feat, nor did it lower the metaphorical altitude of what I was facing. What it did was reassure me that I'd been nearly up that high before.

I am reminded of the command Joshua gave to the Israelites while crossing the Jordan. He told them to reach down and pick up stones from the dry ground God provided (Josh. 4:4–9). The Jordan, I'm guessing from all the anxiety these guys had in getting across, was no bubbling creek. It's described at "flood stage," and I imagine it like a raging river—the kind of river crossing we associate with Wild

West pioneer movies. Panicking livestock and carts barely escaping being carried off over falls, etc.

Pause in the middle of a miraculous, supernatural river dissection, where the water should be washing us downstream but isn't, and pick up a souvenir? Was he *nuts?*

Not at all. Joshua understood that facing the danger and pulling every lesson you can from it is the foundation for courage. Memorializing it if you have to—building an altar from the stones gathered in mortal danger—permits you to trust. It reminded the Israelites to trust God's provision in getting them to the Promised Land.

The knowledge that you were able to get through *that* (whatever *that* was for you), helps you believe you stand a good chance of getting through whatever's coming next. It starts with little stuff like walking and then riding a two-wheel bike. Then it goes on to walking home from school by yourself, taking your first trip alone, facing illness, getting fired from your job, giving birth, the death of a parent or spouse—the list is as long as a life.

A journal can be your own personal pile of Jordan stones. When I am in a state of fear, I have learned to grab pen and paper and write it all down. Tell the page why I'm frightened, what doom I'm sure is going to come, all the gory details. But that's only half the story. It's important that I write the resolution to those fears. How things weren't nearly as bad as I thought, and how there wasn't as much cause for fear as I imagined. Writing the story of my challenges and their solutions can remind me as effectively as Jeff's number one. Facing the dentist chair can remind me I might have what it takes to face the surgeon's knife. Living through my child's kindergarten shots can remind me I can get my little guy through a tonsillectomy. Supporting my fifth grader through her first D on a test—in which case I was surprised to discover it was a close call who cried more—can help me know I can get her through a broken heart some day.

Our children need failures, challenges, and pain to grow. When that seems hard to recognize, think back to your childhood neighborhood. Everyone can usually remember the one overprotected child on the block. The pale, skinny kid whose mother never let him out, who had a dozen suspected allergies, who never got to go on camping trips or buy a skateboard. The one whose mother made him wear a scarf and mittens in April. Maybe you even were that child. There's a host of fear in that kind of upbringing. Such parenting fails to recognize that some of the best things in life involve taking risks, getting messy, and even getting hurt.

We made fun of that overprotective mother when we were young. Now, though, we see bits and pieces (or even huge chunks) of her in our own urge to protect. We don't want our children to endure the worst. It hurts to watch. We fear they won't recover.

But *they can't learn to recover if they don't get the opportunity to recover.* What does not kill them will indeed make them stronger. We need to trust that God meant what he said when he promised not to send us more than we can bear. My daughter learned valuable lessons by scratching and clawing her way back from that really bad grade. I realize, now, that she may have learned more from that gut-wrenching semester than the whole string of As and Bs she normally brings home. You can bet, though, that there are a whole host of journal pages bemoaning that little episode.

> We don't want our children to endure the worst. It hurts to watch. We fear they won't recover. But they can't learn to recover if they don't get the opportunity to recover.

The prophet Ezra spent most of his time reminding Israel how God had protected his chosen people in the past. You'd think that a nation delivered through an epic show of plagues and parting seas wouldn't show a lot of fear at the prospect of rebuilding their temple in hostile territory. Sure, the natives weren't exactly pleased at their new Israelite neighbors, but God could be trusted to protect his people. Their courage came from Ezra's continual reminding. The stories of past deliverance helped the Israelites find courage for the present.

Your journal, your friends, your family, your God can do the same for you. You've been there, you've done that, remember?

Fear-Facing Questions

What are your Jordan stones? What are your stories of survival and overcoming obstacles? How can you use these to bolster your courage today?

Fear Fighter

Write your own personal version of John F. Kennedy's *Profiles in Courage*. Put down on paper the times you have endured, overcome, stood firm, or faced down a fear. Writing those stories out when you are feeling calm and confident gives you a way to remind yourself when you are scared and weak. While you're at it, make one for each of your children to bolster their courage as well.

Faith-Finding Verse

The Lord himself goes before you and will be with you; he will never leave you nor forsake you. Do not be afraid; do not be discouraged.

Deuteronomy 31:8

High Up Is a Long Way to Fall

It's not really the height we fear. There's nothing intrinsically wrong with altitude. If you could magically convince me that there was no way my children could fall, I wouldn't mind how high up off the ground they might be playing. It's what has let me allow my little ones to crawl yards over my head in those playground tubes at McDonald's.

Altitude doesn't automatically mean danger. Challenges, injuries, and setbacks in life don't automatically mean danger. Yet we moms spend so much energy fearing just those things. We fear what's not really dangerous, leaving us with less time, energy, and focus to cope with dangers that are real.

If there are things that could truly take my son's life or destroy his soul, why am I so worried about a broken arm? Truth is, it's *easier* to worry about a broken arm. It's fixable. For many of us, it's an experience we know. It's commonplace, surmountable. It's so much scarier to contemplate what could be the "big fall" in our child's life. Why? Because unlike mending a broken arm, we can't make abuse or addiction or corruption "all better." And that's mighty frightening. We do ourselves an enormous disservice, though, to sweat the small stuff and ignore the major dangers at our heels.

Our love for our children gives us an outstanding ability to perceive their true threats, and our role as mothers gives us unique opportunities to forge relationships that can overcome a lifetime's worth of challenges. God has already given us the best fear fighter in the business: love. Reshape fear's energy into a call to forge the best possible relationships with your children, to love them still harder, still more. And can you think of anyone more qualified to love our children still harder, still more, than their mother? If love is the answer, then we're marvelously qualified.

Love *is* the answer because love, in all it's forms and manifestations, is fear's greatest enemy. First John 4:18 puts it better than I ever could: "Perfect love drives out fear." Sure, moms aren't perfect. But we have the market cornered on love.

Chapter 5

THE BALANCE POLE

"I know it sounds ridiculous, but any time one of my boys does something dumb, I immediately worry that we've uncovered a mental disability."

"When my children are even a minute or two late coming home, I fear that something has happened to them."

"I'm really afraid of germs on hotel bedspreads. Is that crazy, or what?"

It's All Hanging in the Balance

It comes as no surprise that one of the key skills needed to walk a high wire is balance. On the wire, you need to have enough of an innate sense of balance to tolerate being constantly off balance. Rather like standing—you can't successfully attempt standing on one foot until you've mastered staying upright on two feet. On the wire, you are forced to continually adapt to the opposing forces of gravity pulling you to either side of that narrow cable. There is no still, focused place of balance. Instead, you are forever adjusting toward the middle, attempting to orchestrate the workable union of opposing forces.

Parenthood's constant compensation is no different. No rule, no guideline, no strategy lasts for long—parenthood is the ongoing process of readjustment. New ages, new factors, new challenges, and new threats rise up daily. Like walking the high wire, courageous parenting is achieved by the workable union of the opposing forces. Only our two forces aren't the double sides of gravity, they are the opposing forces of protection and preparation. These two concepts—protection and preparation—are seemingly at war with each other in the heart of every parent. If I let them risk, they can grow. If I let them risk, they can be hurt. Tension, tension.

> These two concepts—protection and preparation—are seemingly at war with each other in the heart of every parent. If I let them risk, they can grow. If I let them risk, they can be hurt.

Opposing forces, however, *do* create balance. Think of antique scales—not the kind from the bathroom floor that digitally remind you how much you blew your diet, but the ones with two dishes hanging on either side of a pole. The kind Lady Justice carries. Equal amounts of weight on both sides achieve balance. The trick comes in knowing how to keep that weight equal on both sides.

Aerialists take it a step further, scientifically, to look at what's known as their center of gravity. The lower your center of gravity, the less gravity tugs you to one side or another, and the less likely you are to fall. Think of a block tower. The taller you make it, the more easily it will fall. Aerialists' balance has nothing to do with how high they are off the ground. The pole system they use to keep them upright would work just as easily one foot in the air as four stories up. That's because your center of gravity comes from *inside you*, not your situation. It's internal, not external.

As mothers, the external forces at play in our lives wield just as much force as gravity. Some days the threats facing our children, the perceived odds of successfully raising happy, healthy adults, and the worry that we'll never get our act together all feel as insurmountable as the force of gravity. To fight against this, a mother needs her own center of gravity, her own solid core, in order to find the balance she needs.

Every human being has a center of gravity; it's just that many of us who don't do acrobatics on a regular basis haven't honed the skills of using it. Your core, your emotional center that you can wield in the face of fear, already exists. It's just that we mothers often don't have the time, energy, or space to hone its use. Go at this balancing act of motherhood gracefully? Forget it. We spend most of our days just trying to stay upright.

There's no mistaking how much fear is piled up on one side of those scales. What do we fill the other side with to balance it out? That's a powerful question—and one we all too often ignore.

I believe we can fight fear with three weapons—three weights, if you will, to put on the scale opposite all that heavy fear. They are perspective, companionship, and humor. These are the secrets to balance on the high wire of motherhood.

Challenge 1:
We Fear Far Beyond the Facts
Jumping to Inconclusions

Life seems ready—even eager—to knock us off balance. Especially when we're already wobbly. The minute one child gets over an illness, like clockwork another one presents symptoms. One teenage problem ebbs while another kicks into high gear. Just as we get our kids on good footing, our elderly parents go to pieces. We're so busy dealing with crisis number one that crisis number two has an easy shot.

We want to solve *each* crisis, pour ourselves into making it *all* better. It's no wonder, then, that things get out of whack. When you're already caught off balance, your reaction to a crisis—or even something that just *looks* like a crisis—comes off-kilter too.

When Christopher was a newborn, he gave us quite a scare. CJ, it seems, hadn't caught on that breathing was an important part of life outside the womb. So he spent his first days in neonatal intensive care and was the recipient of a fair amount of medical intervention. I'll admit, that's enough to make any mother nervous—even if it is her second child. He's completely fine now, and we've never uncovered any ill effects from his rather dramatic entrance into this world. But as you can imagine, they ran *dozens* of tests in his first month of life.

> Life seems ready—even eager—to knock us off balance. Especially when we're already wobbly. We're so busy dealing with crisis number one that crisis number two has an easy shot.

My mother was visiting, allowing me to catch a much-needed nap (colic—need I say more?). The doctor's office phoned and made it quite clear that Mom needed to wake me up to hear some test results. She handed me the phone, trying to look calm. The doctor's office informed me that one of CJ's tests had come back "inconclusive." That's medical for "something may be up but we're not sure yet." I no longer even remember what the test was, only that it had something to do with CJ's cognitive abilities.

This was a touchy subject for me. Of all the potential outcomes of CJ's oxygen deprivation, a cognitive disability was the one I wasn't sure I could handle. My professional life in fundraising had led me to work in a disability rights organization, so I was actually quite comfortable with the idea of coping with a physical disability if it came to that. But something to do with his brain—oh, that idea scared the pants off me.

My reaction far exceeded the danger at hand. It was far too soon to get worried, but you can bet that didn't stop me. My balance had already been thrown way off by the physical stresses of a colicky newborn, too little sleep, more stitches than an entire Civil War battalion, and roller coaster hormones. Not to mention a whole host of other emotional issues like leaving my career to become a stay-at-home mom and having my visiting mother suffer a heart attack in the airport (another *very* long story).

I had no balance. Not a shred. And this new wrinkle became the thing that teetered me over the edge. I cried. I wailed. Visions of special schools, every negative stereotype you can imagine, medications, inappropriate public behavior, Dustin Hoffman in *Rain Man*, it all swam through my head within minutes of the news. I shook my fist at the heavens for a God who would heap such a load onto me. In short, I lost it.

Losing it, under stressful circumstances, is a very human, very natural reaction. We all need to lose it from time to time. We need to react, to stomp and scream and moan and let it out.

But then we need to get up again. I had lost that ability. This minor test took over my life for the next couple of days. Here's one situation where I think the Internet is not our friend. We can access way too much information without having the perspective to interpret it wisely. One phrase into an Internet search engine and we have 167 conflicting references. We have the full spectrum of possibility without any hint of probability—from people we've never met and have no idea if we can trust.

Here I was, fortifying myself to be the mother of a mentally challenged child, listing all the potential outcomes of this test, and sending my blood pressure through the ceiling. I was already in a situation in which I needed my wits about me, and I was tossing my wits out the window and welcoming panic in through the front door.

> One phrase into an Internet search engine and we have 167 conflicting references. We have the full spectrum of possibility without any hint of probability—from people we've never met and have no idea if we can trust.

You can't help but act this way when you spend so much of your time at your wit's end. The first decade of motherhood is a season of life when babies and people and physical stress and changing relationships push us to our limits. Each of us has gone off the deep end at one time or another about one issue or another. Parenthood hands us infinite reasons—and infinite opportunities—to lose our perspective and overreact like this.

It was not the facts, but my imbalance that skewed my focus on that one detail. I let one of the opposing forces in my life pull me overboard. In reality, all that phone call communicated was a need to retake the test, using a more sensitive version to give more detailed results. The doctor's office had insisted I be woken up because there are state laws that demand they be able to document informing the parent. Granted, it's cruel to wake a sleeping new mother, but you can't blame them. It wasn't the major issue I made it out to be. I had lost my balance.

There was no way to change that situation. Those tests had to be done. Those possibilities had to be considered. It would have been better for everyone, though, if I had found a more effective way to cope.

How? Much of what I was facing was in the hands of the diagnostic equipment, not my abilities. Well, yes and no. What was still in my control, and will always be within my control, was *my choice of reactions*. My decision whether to jump to inconclusions.

The best lesson I know for this comes from an unlikely source: river rafting. My friend Julie told me about a white-water rafting trip she took. The trip was exhilarating and fun, but the potent truth she took away from the experience was not what you'd expect. It came from a nugget of instruction her river guide gave her.

You see, when you're paddling down the river and you see a threat such as a submerged rock, waterfall, enormous, hungry-looking bear on the shore, or whatever, it's not wise to point at it to warn your fellow paddlers. Why? If you *point* at the danger, then everyone *looks* at the danger, which makes them start *drifting towards* the danger while they're busy looking, and, well, you can guess the rest.

Instead, you're supposed to do something called "point positive." That means you point not to the danger but to the *safety*. You point to the side of the river without the submerged boulder. You point to the shoreline ahead of the rapids. You point to the opposite shore of the hungry bear.

In essence, you force your focus to the *solution*, not the problem. That doesn't mean it's not wise to know that a bear is there; it just means you're far better off training your view on the opposite shore.

How could I point positive in CJ's test situation? For one thing, I could fire up my support group of other moms and friends to help me get the sleep and fellowship I needed to react more calmly. Being with those people—instead of hunkering down with my medical texts of doom—can remind me of my skills as a mother rather than of the enormity of the problem. I can look at how carefully my pediatrician is monitoring CJ and try to muster up a little gratitude for all the medical science that saved him in the first place. I can look at my son, notice how he reacts to me, how his movements seem natural and unhampered for a baby his age. I can ask God for the eyes to see all the positive, the ears to hear all the compliments, and the faith to receive all the reassurance that things stand a good chance of coming out okay.

Things, however, may not come out okay, and I'd be foolish to deny that. So I must face my fear that I won't be able to cope. I must fill the opposite side of *that* scale, as well. I can ask people for my own Jordan River stones—to tell me why they think I can cope and recount instances in which I've coped well. I can talk to people who have faced a similar situation and learn how God helped them through it. All these things would refocus my attention and point positive toward the solution, not the problem.

If you are facing a major fear, see if you can't turn it into a major challenge. The larger your fear, the more you'll need to focus your effort and attention on the positive. You need to ensure that you are piling up as much weight as you need on the positive side of that scale. If it's a monster of a problem, you need an even bigger dose of reassurance.

Don't kid yourself—this doesn't come easily. It will take some effort on your part to change the natural course of your thinking. You'll have to make a deliberate effort to pull your deer-in-headlights gaze off the crisis and make yourself look toward a solution.

When her therapy clients deal with this issue, Ms. Gresko asks them an astoundingly useful question: "How much time do you want to spend each day thinking about this?" I was struck by its powerful simplicity. No one really wants to spend hours agonizing over something, but we seem to automatically assume there's nothing to be done about it. I mean, there's this horrible fear right in our faces, and it isn't going to go away soon. So what's to be done? Gresko's technique draws the fine but useful distinction between "don't worry about it" and "don't worry about it every waking moment."

Choose an amount of time, says Gresko, and let yourself have that time of worry. Sit and stew, write it all down, hash it out on the phone with a friend. You may have to allow a lot of time at first. Then, you may choose to slowly whittle it down as you get your feet underneath you regarding the issue. But when that set time is up, call yourself on it. Say to yourself—out loud if you need to, for that seems to be effective—"I'm done worrying about that for today. I need to move on to something else." Then do so.

If you're like me, though, there will be a "good mother" voice saying, "It's not solved. You can't stop worrying about this. You're just walking away from the problem and no good mother would do that." Gresko would tell us we're simply recognizing the weight of the pole we're holding, coming to grips with the irreconcilable tension that is motherhood: Life is good, God is trustworthy, but nothing is truly safe. The powerful truth is that *giving yourself more time for fear and worry will not help the situation.* What will help is getting yourself to move on so you can gather some of the perspective that might point you to good solutions.

Now is no time to be shy—get a different friend to call you each day of the week if you have to. I enlisted the help of my family while facing down the barrel of this book's deadline, and I asked *each of them* to tell me *every day* that I could do it. Three time a day I hear, "You can do it!"—like emotional vitamins.

You may want to start what author Diane Eble calls an "Abundant Gifts" journal[9] and make a point of writing down the good gifts that come to you each day. Look everywhere—from the brilliant fall colors to the great hint in the women's magazine you happened to pick up in the doctor's office. Ask every friend you know to list your gifts, talents, and strengths and why you've got what it takes to make it through this.

Most of all, remember you've got *who it takes.* The Lord of the universe. God Almighty, who was, and is, and is to come. I especially like the following advice someone gave me: "Do not tell God what enormous problems you have, but tell your problems what an enormous God you have."

> *The powerful truth is that giving yourself more time for fear and worry will not help the situation. What will help is getting yourself to move on so you can gather some of the perspective that might point you to good solutions.*

Fear-Facing Questions

Where in your parenting are you currently "jumping to inconclusions"? Is it helpful? Why is it making things worse? Where is a better place for your mental and emotional focus?

Fear Fighter

Ask yourself, "How much time do I want to spend today worrying about this?" Set a time and then stick to it. Tell yourself, out loud if necessary, that you're done worrying about it for today. Then move on to something else in any way you can.

Faith-Finding Verse

Preserve sound judgment and discernment, do not let them out of your sight; they will be life for you, an ornament to grace your neck. Then you will go on your way in safety, and your foot will not stumble; when you lie down, you will not be afraid; when you lie down, your sleep will be sweet. Have no fear of sudden disaster or of the ruin that overtakes the wicked, for the Lord will be your confidence and will keep your foot from being snared.

Proverbs 3:21–26

Challenge 2:
We Fear Little Problems into Big Ones

*It's Easy to Supersize Your Fears in the
Incredible Shrinking Mommy World*

Some days, staying part of the big, wide world is like being a salmon swimming *up* Niagara Falls. Moms everywhere are fighting a powerful current just to get out the door. How easily we forget that such isolation exacts a heavy price.

Valentine's Day 2003, for example, was not a pinnacle of romance at the Pleiter household. No ma'am, we marked that holiday as day eleven of the flu. My daughter had missed eight days of school; my son had missed six. I was on day eleven of Mommy House Arrest. I missed the outside world more than the Man in the Iron Mask. To top things off, we had just learned that CJ not only had the flu but had developed pneumonia.

Want to talk fear? Normally I like to think of myself as a medically calm mother, but you use a word like *pneumonia* and I go a little crazy. Pneumonia is one of those things that can *kill* people. Yes, we caught it early, and he was doing well and in no real danger now that he was under treatment. But, well, it's *pneumonia*. I did fine for a couple of hours—after all, we kept busy with trips to the pharmacy and calls to friends to bring over their entire video collection as we had been instructed to keep CJ quiet for at least four days.

Keep CJ *quiet?* Oh yes, doctor, there's an easy task. Especially when his big sister is cranky from battling her own flu, ear infection, and sinus infection.

My world was placed in not-so-solitary confinement. I couldn't leave the house because CJ wasn't supposed to go outside, and he wasn't old enough to be left alone for any length of time. During night number twelve, I watched the syndrome I call "the Incredible Shrinking Mommy World" spring into action. America was on the brink of war. That was the week they were telling us to buy plastic sheeting and duct tape. They were showing pictures of armed guards in New York's Grand Central Station. I was fondly remembering the times the phrases "red alert" and "yellow alert" were only things on *Star Trek*. Some guy was telling us the economy was about to take the nosedive of a lifetime. My brother and his family—the only members of my immediate family I have left—live in that big fat target called Washington, D.C. I was freaking out.

As I helped Christopher through a coughing jag at 1:30 a.m., you could have convinced me in a heartbeat that life itself was coming to an end. I was scared for my son. Scared for my family. Scared for the economy, my husband's job, and our life savings. Scared for my nation, my own health, the national water supply. You name it, I was scared about it. Stuff that normally wouldn't rattle me had me shaking in my jammies.

Why? For starters, there *was* a lot to be scared of in the world then. Anytime someone starts telling me to buy water and canned goods, I'm entitled to get a little nervous. Especially since I couldn't even leave my house to buy those disaster preparedness goods anyway. Oh no, we'd die instead from starvation because I couldn't make it out of the house to the 7-Eleven to stock up on Spam.

Enter dawn, coffee, and a dose of reality. In the light of day I realized that much of my hysteria was driven by the skewed focus of eleven days at home with sick kids. I could look at the things that were frightening me and tell myself that while there is reason for concern, my level of panic was more about my *situation* than about the problem. I could recognize that until things lightened up, the TV news probably wasn't the best place for my focus right then. When isolated like that, I'm far better off sticking to the newspaper, where I can still stay informed but not get so sucked in emotionally. Claiming my situation as part of the problem was no magic cure, but it did help to be able to tell myself that

> Claiming my situation as part of the problem was no magic cure, but it did help to be able to tell myself that at least a portion of what I was feeling wasn't real.

at least a *portion* of what I was feeling wasn't real.

Every mother has been through some similar confinement. While it does seem to be the most intense when our children are very young, it never really stops. The natural spiral of a mother's life curves inward, homeward. That's a good thing; our children and our home deserve the best of our attentions. But it can allow little problems to escalate very quickly into big ones. Head lice seems like the end of the known universe if you're not careful. Now head lice is one of childhood's champion yukkies, but it's not a crisis of gargantuan proportions. Try telling that, though, to a mother of a third grader who is on her twenty-seventh load of hot-water laundry.

Mothers of young children aren't the only ones whose lives turn inward. I'm reminded of a dear friend whose father was in his last days. This man was a great thinker— a college professor, a man of large and complicated ideas. His exceptional mind dwelt on theology you and I may never have the chance to contemplate. Yet as his body began to fail him, his world spiraled inward. The challenges of daily living eventually eclipsed the great truths he used to ponder. Eventually, he never left the house, then never left his bed. Like our new mother, his life became more and more about mundane chores of physical care, pure daily survival. When my friend bemoaned to her mother the loss of her dad's intellectual prowess, the mother said something very wise. "Dear," she said, "that's just how small his world has become."

Crises, like death and birth, pull our world inward. Yes, there's a certain degree to which that tight focus is a necessity, as it boils the complications of life down to the real, important truths. But it can also be the enemy. Cancer patients are often encouraged not to make fighting cancer their career—not to let the rigors of their treatment eclipse the other parts of their lives. Not that it won't sometimes, no matter what they do. But they are encouraged to at least make a deliberate fight against it taking over their lives.

So how did I keep the specter of Mandy's illness and CJ's pneumonia from taking over my life? You can bet your amoxicillin (and my fridge was full of it, let me tell you) that I got on my phone. I talked to as many friends as I could. (Cordless headset phones in your kitchen are a godsend at times like these!) I made a conscious effort to connect in every way I could with the world outside my quarantined front door.

It helps, then, to *have* a full life. As mothers, our world tends to shrink. It's hard to remember there's a whole world outside the front door when it takes you twenty-seven minutes just to get your baby's clothes on and you're often still in your pajamas at lunch. Life boils down to the very basics—diapers, feedings, sleeping, changing linens—when a new baby comes. I know people who intentionally don't take a baby out of the house for the first thirty days! We must, though, recognize the dangers in that isolation. I believe mothers need to push against the limitations of our world, fight to keep it wide, and be deliberate about maintaining the connections that will help us keep balance.

Think outside your home. Get outside your home. Even a cup of coffee at McDonald's with another mom and her cranky baby can do the trick. Nurture your roles of citizen, woman, wife, best friend, church member, artist, and activist. Realize and take responsibility for the priority of your self-care. Recognize that your health—spiritually, physically, emotionally—dictates how well you can care for others. In short, take care of yourself!

> *It's hard to remember there's a whole world outside the front door when it takes you twenty–seven minutes just to get your baby's clothes on and you're often still in your pajamas at lunch.*

I was better off that morning because I had friendships that I've spent time nurturing. I had friends to call. I had hobbies to occupy my time and connections on which to capitalize when things get hairy. But I had to *make those things happen* in my life—they didn't materialize on their own. And they are strong lifelines, wise investments.

If you are in a tight spot, make the following list of people with whom to connect. Try to talk to as many of them as you can during your crisis. Their help will be invaluable in keeping your balance and pointing you toward a useful solution:

1. Someone who really likes you.
2. Someone you admire.
3. Someone who's been through your situation and overcome it, or is at least coping well with it.
4. Someone who is going through a similar situation.
5. Someone who is just plain funny.
6. Someone with whom you've been wanting to start a friendship but haven't yet.
7. An old friend with whom you've lost touch.
8. Someone whose situation is worse than yours.
9. Someone who has something practical you need (like videos, a baby gate, crutches, etc.).
10. Someone who can pray for you.

You may not get through all ten phone calls, but just knowing that there are people out there who can help you is often encouragement enough. Look at that list and say a prayer that God will lead you to those people, that he'll provide the time and energy to make those calls, and that he'll send you the help and lifelines you need.

We're talking about the God who parented an entire nation of whiny Israelites through forty years of desert wandering. He understands. And I have a feeling God knows what you need to help you make it through the chicken pox.

Fear-Facing Questions

How isolated have you become as a mother? Do you have a group of friends on whom you can call when things get tight? If not, what can you do to widen your circle of support?

Fear Fighter

Connect with your world when isolation breeds fear. Make a list of ten people who can serve as a resource— emotional, spiritual, or practical—and call them. And don't forget to nurture your relationships in times of calm so that they are strong in times of chaos.

Faith-Finding Verse

Who of you by worrying can add a single hour to his life?

Luke 12:25

Challenge 3:
We Fear When We Can Only See Darkness
The World's Most Welcome Box of Snacks

Sometimes life hands us a moment so dark we have no idea if we'll ever see light again. It is then that we must rely on God to send us someone with a very big lantern. And he will.

When my mother was found dead of a heart attack in her own home, it was a tremendous shock to everyone. Even though she'd had her share of health problems in her final years, she had been in good health in the months before her death. Her sudden death left everyone scrambling to cope—emotionally and logistically.

I was determined to give the eulogy at my mother's funeral. With all the public speaking in my background, I didn't see how I could let this important opportunity pass me by. I saw it as a chance to put a fine and noble cap on a relationship that had been deep but challenging. Still, this would be a hugely difficult task. I wasn't the least bit sure I could pull it off.

While planning the funeral, I called my college roommate Melissa for support because she had lost her mother years earlier. As we commiserated, Melissa asked me what I thought it would take to make it through the next few days. "Prayer, coffee, my brother, and the world's largest box of Yodels," was my desperately joking answer.

You see, Yodels are a Ho-Ho-like chocolate snack food you can only get on the East Coast, where I grew up. I love Yodels. My first stop anytime I head back east is to the grocery store for a box of Yodels. To me, Yodels are the stuff of sticky-fingered childhood, lovingly packed lunch boxes, and trips to the dime store for a goody after church on Sundays. Comfort junk food, if you will.

By the time of the funeral, I was running on grief and adrenaline. The long timeframe between Mom's death and the discovery of her body (she lived alone and both my brother and I lived some distance from her) led the funeral director to recommend that we not view the body. The lack of physical evidence by which to process such a stressful event made it strangely unrealistic, incomprehensible, even spooky.

Somehow during all the visitations and preparations, and without even realizing it, I had managed never to touch the casket. Just before we moved it to the church for the funeral, though, I laid my hand on it. To say goodbye I suppose, to put closure on the life of my last surviving parent. When my hand hit the smooth wood, my heart exploded without warning. Everything about this surreal experience became horribly, instantly concrete. I was touching *my mother's casket.* A coffin that would sink irrevocably into the ground mere hours from now. My mother was dead.

A deep, dark fear gripped me. I was suddenly terrified of life without any parents at all. Terrified that I'd go to pieces in front of all my mother's dearest friends. Terrified that I'd made a foolish, self-indulgent choice to try and speak at her funeral. Fearful that I was destined for the same early death so many in my family had known. I stood there paralyzed, racked with emotion, exhausted, and choking back waves upon waves of panic and tears. I remember just trying to breathe and stay upright as Jeff piloted me out into the car and down the street to her church.

As I got out of the car in front of the church, my one thought was that I simply did not possess enough composure to go through with this. Truly, I thought I was going to faint. Noble or indulgent, this opportunity to honor my mother was going to pass me by—understandably, but regrettably. I could not pull this off.

Then I looked up at the church steps. Melissa and her husband were waiting there, standing where I'd be sure to see them. In possession—I would soon learn—of an absolutely gigantic box of Yodels. I have never been so happy to see anyone. I laughed through my tears that Melissa had made the effort to be there for me and for her knowledge that something as absurd as Yodels would give me the foothold to make it through that day.

And I did make it. I gave the speech of a lifetime and listened in awe as my brother did the same. Someone even remarked that he had never heard a woman so eloquently eulogized by not one but both of her children. It was a moment I will always hold near to my heart.

That experience was a valuable lesson in the power of laughter to get us through life's darkest moments. Laughter kept me from losing that irrecoverable chance. Laughter is a way to find balance when the whole world seems ready to push us off our feet.

We need to laugh—well and often. Laugh at the things that scare you if you can, and if you can't, then laugh at the Three Stooges.

> We need to laugh—well and often. Laugh at the things that scare you if you can, and if you can't, then laugh at the Three Stooges.

Okay, now wait a minute—I don't know too many women who find the Three Stooges funny. It seems to be a uniquely guy thing. I look at their antics and stare blankly while my husband guffaws on the couch. Write me if you can explain this phenomenon.

So maybe you need to find your own funnymen. But you get the point: Laughing at anything battles fear. Laughing at something inherently funny is a good and healthy thing. Even more powerful, though, is the ability to laugh at something about the fearful situation in which you find yourself. Laughter, even if it must be through tears, is one of life's most powerful healers.

Why do you think many people laugh when they're nervous? It is a natural tension releaser. According to recent medical studies, laughter is also chemically healthy. The physical act of laughter activates the immune system, decreases stress hormones such as epinephrine and cortisol, releases pain-fighting endorphins, and is actually good aerobic exercise.

Think your situation is too dark to host a funny bone? Rent the movie *Life is Beautiful* (PG–13) at the video store. Be warned: You'll need a box of tissues. Roberto Benigni gives an extraordinary performance as the clownlike father who somehow finds within himself the means to inject humor and amusement into a Nazi death camp. You see him struggle, toiling to find ways to reshape the horrors of war to help his wife and child cope. Benigni's character's victory is bittersweet, and it comes at a painfully dear cost. But it shows us that finding the humor in a situation— even if you have to look really, *really* hard—is the ultimate enforcer of "it can't be that bad."

It is a tremendous gift to be able to dig the humor out of a dark moment, but not everyone has such a gift. If you're not an inherently funny person, make friends with someone who is—your own Melissa with your own personally tailored box of Yodels. Even if you are a funny person, gather some funny friends around you because there will be times when you are too flooded with the darkness to find the lighter side of things.

I am frequently heard to say something along the lines of, "God must have a sense of humor because. . . " I believe it to be true. Our God is not just a God of power and might but of love and light, of laughter and joy. And he certainly must have a funny bone. One need only consider the aardvark and the platypus as evidence. Can you ask such a God to send you a chuckle in the middle of a crisis? You betcha. In fact, God knows, better than anyone on the planet, what exact brand of humor you need at even the darkest moment. He's just waiting for you to ask.

Or God may send you as the bearer of light to someone else. Go there. Be there. Laugh.

Fear-Facing Questions

Are you in a dark and humorless place right now? Who can you call on to bring humor into your life? Think of the funniest person you know and bring him or her into your life. If you are a funny gal, who might need your special brand of joy today?

Fear Fighter

Ask six people you know to name the funniest movie or person they know. Keep a list. When you are in a dark place, call that person or rent the movie. Buy a joke book. Spend ten minutes making silly faces with your kids. It doesn't have to have anything to do with your current situation— any good laugh will do.

Faith-Finding Verse

When I said, "My foot is slipping," your love, O Lord, supported me. When anxiety was great within me, your consolation brought joy to my soul.
Psalm 94:18–19

Balance Is Far from Easy

Most people think of a guy holding a long pole when they picture someone on the high wire. They're right; a pole is one of the most essential pieces of high-wire equipment. I had no idea, though, how difficult it is to hold an aerialist's pole. It is heavy—between thirty and forty pounds by necessity—and cumbersome. It takes training, strength, and determination to wield that pole up on the wire.

Self-care for mothers is no different. Just as gravity would coax us to drop a forty-pound pole, the demands of our lives coax us to drop those things that give us balance. It is easy to stay home and not get out to see people. It is easier not to step out of your comfort zone to make new friends or find a support group. It is easier not to carve out time in your day to read or knit or work in your garden. It is cheaper not to hire a sitter so you can get away. I've found it to be a battle to keep those kinds of things in my schedule.

Remember, then, that those aerialists who drop their poles *will surely fall.* It's worth the effort to keep that pole in your hands.

The same is true of mothering in scary times. Keeping an even keel—having that sense of grace and calm we think mothers are supposed to have—feels like it will require some enormous, effective tool. The thirst for balance, for the ability to move past "stagger and survive" to "walk forward and thrive" runs deep in every mother. We yearn to feel good about what we do. To feel as though we're making wise choices, to know we're giving our parenting the attention and effort it deserves. To find parenting peace of mind.

Balance is difficult to achieve when we feel like a dozen demands and concerns are pulling and pushing us off the path to piece of mind. We seek to feel grounded. We wish for a confidence that seems to linger forever just out of reach. *I might be able to be a good mother,* we think, *if I could just get over the sensation that my next step is going to be a doozy.*

Perhaps, then, we should retrain our thoughts. Perhaps it might be better to accept that most parenting steps *are* doozies. It's an illusion to pretend that the fear isn't there. It *is* there. And it's not going to go away. I've been a parent twelve years now, and the fear hasn't subsided yet—but it's balanced. I've slowly developed an ability to hold fear in the proper perspective. When more fear piles up on one side of the balance, I know to pile up more support, humor, and positive pointing on the other side. I find it more helpful to cope with my fears this way than to spend time and energy trying to make them go away.

> When more fear piles up on one side of the balance, I know to pile up more support, humor, and positive pointing on the other side.

Since fears won't just go away, the best I can shoot for is to have them subside into balance. But balance doesn't descend on you from on high; you have to carve it out of the opposing forces around you. Yes, I believe you can ask God to send you what you need to find balance, and he can certainly send you peace, but you're going to have to find balance on your own.

Never forget that when you cry out to God that one side of your life is about to pull you over, he hears you. He sends you an experience, a thought, a person, or even a box of Yodels that wields just the right force in the opposite direction.

You can bet your balance on it.

Chapter 6

TAKING STEPS

*"I can't let my six-year-old on the bus.
I'm afraid something bad will happen to him."*

*"I fear letting my children go to college. I don't think
I've prepared them for life's pressures. And I'm afraid
I'll miss them so much and discover I don't really have
a good relationship with my husband once
it's just the two of us."*

*"I already worry about my girls dating.
They're only two and four."*

How Do We Keep Moving Forward on This Journey?

You have to walk the wire if you're ever going to make it to the other side. An aerialist has a better chance of staying balanced when he or she is moving forward. As a matter of fact, as an aerialist-in-training, I had to be continually in the process of walking. If I stood still on the wire I would fall. I needed all three available limbs—both arms and the other leg—to keep my balance. So to stay upright, I had to keep taking another step forward.

I really thought the high wire was going to be about still, balletic movements. It wasn't. You can make it look still and graceful if you're a real expert, but it is really about constant motion, constant adjustment, constantly proceeding forward.

In this respect, it reminded me of a two-wheel bicycle—the forward momentum is crucial to keeping you upright. If you've ever tried to ride your own bicycle behind that of your new-to-the-two-wheeler child, you know that you end up going so slow you can barely keep your own bike upright. You need the little guy to go faster if you want to have an easier time on your own bike.

But stop right there. Here's a microcosm of the motherhood fear factor. If your little guy goes faster, he might fall. He might get hurt. He might go ahead of you too far and turn the corner so you can't see him, and then he'll surely be abducted just like you saw on last night's news. Sound familiar? I think it's why I insisted my husband teach our little ones how to ride a two-wheeler. I haven't the nerves of steel it requires. Now, of course, we have to face teaching our oldest to drive in five short years. I'm not sure either of us has calm enough nerves for that.

Fear can be about motion—the old "fight or flight" principle—but I find more often it's about paralysis. If I'm frightened, I can't move, because any move I might make could be the wrong one and make things worse. Then, of course, I'm free to sit stewing in my terror and dream up a thousand new reasons to be even more scared.

Fear chokes our ability to see, to identify even the smallest of improvements available to us. When under siege it is so easy to convince ourselves that there is simply nothing that can be done. That it is hopeless and we have been rendered helpless. Worst of all, it doesn't seem to take a catastrophe to accomplish this. Women, especially mothers, can let our potent imaginations hold us hostage in even the smallest of crises. Why? Because we are the first to conjure up the ramifications, to imagine the lifetime scars any given event will hold.

It doesn't even take human crisis for me to react in fear. If the heater goes down and I'm stuck at home waiting for a repairman when I needed to be out getting things done, I respond by sitting in the middle of my kitchen floor and pronouncing the day shot. My husband, on the other hand, can redirect his energies in a heartbeat, dreaming up a list of things he can get done while he's home and putting aside all the outside things that aren't getting done. Not me. It's hard to shake myself out of the stupor of fear and anger. (Of course I'm already thinking about how the cost of the new heater will eat into the funds we've saved for Mandy's orthodontic work.)

I once heard motivational speaker and health-care quality expert John J. Pelizza speak. He related that often patients and their caregivers get caught up in the concept of "making it good." There are situations, such as terminal illness or chronic pain, in which "good" simply isn't achievable. Or at least it is so far off that it's not helpful to talk about now. What is helpful, he said, is to look at making it "better."[10] *Better* implies that we take small steps in the right direction.

I have found this very helpful in facing my fears as a mother. I often cannot make a situation go away. There are times when Mom simply cannot make it *good*. But there is always a way to make it *better*—even if only by a bit.

> There are times where Mom simply cannot make it good. But there is always a way to make it better—even if only by a bit.

I've uncovered some rather inventive ways to achieve that "bit of better." Some are sensible, some make little sense but seem effective anyway. A smart mom will use both kinds of small steps to move herself and her family away from fear. A faithful mom knows she can ask God to reveal such steps to her. You'll be amazed at how we can learn to harness even our physical senses to snap us out of our fear-soaked stupor.

The sure truth is that *any* step in the right direction will reduce fear. So gather up your courage and holler, "Feet, don't fail me now!" because we're stepping out—in faith.

Challenge 1:
We Can Be Frozen with Fear—
and Still Thaw

Even Cold Feet Can Start a Journey with a Single Step

If you stood in a crowded movie theater and asked every person to name the most frightening day they've had in the last three years, I'm betting a large chunk of those answers would be "September 11, 2001." It's been a long time since we could name a day of such potent national fear. For the first time in decades, Americans felt that we were in the global crosshairs. Someone had it in for us. They did us real, lasting harm. That's scary stuff. My response to that day is what planted the first seeds for the book you now hold.

That fateful morning began for me when my husband called me from work and said in a voice I knew was unnatural, "Do you know what's happening?" I don't normally have the television or radio on in the mornings, so I was blissfully unaware. When I replied, "no," he said very quietly, "Turn on the TV."

I clicked the set on in time to watch the second plane hit its tower. From that moment, and for hours afterward, I watched helplessly as the world seemed to crumble before me. We live near Chicago's international airport and are used to seeing airplanes constantly pass overhead. But when I looked up that day, the skies were eerily quiet; it was entirely too real. I walked to the bus stop later that morning to pick up my kindergartner and wondered how on earth I would explain this to him. Then I realized I simply couldn't.

I did not handle that day well. Sucked into the fear of it all, I sat glued to CNN (now suddenly available on network television—we don't have cable). Despite my better judgment that my kindergartner should not be watching this, I watched, and watched, and watched, and watched.

In all honesty, I got so frightened that *my fear began to scare my child.* It was something I'd never experienced before and rather uncharacteristic for me. There was absolutely no way I could make this *good.* The "fixer," the "make it all better mama" in me was as helpless as helpless could be, and it was sucking me under.

Just before my daughter came home from school, though, God gave me the grace to remember a tiny bit of advice I'd heard in my past. I had done some fundraising work for a counseling center, and while I was sitting in the doctor's office, he fielded a call from a woman distraught over her just-finalized divorce. It was a great life lesson to listen to him talk her through the crisis. First, he listened to her. Really, really listened. He let her get some of the raw emotion out. Then, he told her to get up and go outside. "When all else fails," he said, "go outside and take a walk."

> *"When all else fails," he said, "go outside and take a walk."*

It sounded simplistic on the phone, but it is perhaps the most useful bit of crisis management I have ever heard. I followed it when I received the phone call telling me my mother had died. There is power in it; something clarifying happens when we engage our bodies, get out under the sky, and simply move forward.

So on the afternoon of September 11, 2001, with body counts running at the bottom of the screen as CNN blared through my TV, with planes silenced overhead, and with relatives across the country phoning loved ones to see if they were all right, I took my five-year-old son for a walk. That walk became a gift from God—a foothold against the growing terror. Why? Because on that walk, I forced myself to look up and see the sky as September's uniquely crisp style of sunny beauty, not as vacant and under siege. I breathed. I sent the tension in my body out through my legs, not up through my imagination. I held my son's hand.

And we saw a flag. Three or four blocks into our walk, someone had put their flag up on their flagpole. Farther down the block, the idea had caught on and someone else had taped a paper flag in their window. Flag after flag came into view.

I had a little flag at home somewhere that we only pulled out to wave at the Independence Day parade. I'm sure the thing was only about six inches tall, but we had a flag. And by golly, we were going to fly it today.

CJ and I walked home and rummaged through the attic until we found not one but three flags. Sure, it did nothing to bolster national security. And from a purely logical point of view, it was useless. But it was a baby step, a tiny task that could set my emotions in the right direction. I could remember our strength as a nation and put forth this tiny symbol of unity. I don't think I've ever given the U.S. flag a moment of true thought before that day. I'm sorry to say that although our house has had a flagpole for thirteen years, before September 11 I had never owned a full-size American flag.

My son and I planted those flags in the ground of our front lawn with no small amount of ceremony. We made a great big deal out of flying those tiny flags. And that seemingly inconsequential act became an emotional watershed. It gave me the momentum to find something more nurturing to do with my time that day than scan the network news in front of my children. It shook me gently to my senses, if you will. I couldn't make it good, but that flag made it *better*.

One tiny watershed led to another. Instead of sitting around giving in to the rising panic that somehow life would never quite be the same, we began working our way through our repertoire of nurturing, homey activities. We colored on the floor in front of the fireplace. We made chocolate chip cookies. As we mixed batter, we prayed for the nation. We made phone calls, checked in on relatives in my home state of Connecticut, sent emails, said prayers for my friends in Manhattan, and held up our leaders to God for wisdom and strength.

We focused our attention on what we *could* do: We could pray, we could keep panic at bay, and we could make our home a haven from the world's tensions. Sure, there is no logical connection between making cookies and fighting terrorism, but I've discovered it doesn't always have to be logical.

When things look so scary your brain convinces you there's no way out, it's a good sign that you're in the midst of a huge problem with serious implications. Now that sounds obvious when you're dealing with national security, but often problems that *ought* to feel small somehow feel enormous for reasons we can't explain. It is best not to trivialize such an emotion. It is a signal to you that *there is more at stake than you may be ready to admit*. Even if you don't yet fully understand what's making you so panicked, it's important to respect the strength of such emotions.

When you find yourself at the edge of such a panic (or even if you find yourself over that edge), don't waste energy berating your overactive adrenaline. Instead, pull yourself to a complete stop for a moment and ask yourself: "What can I do *today*?" All too often our brains immediately jump to huge, complicated *solutions*—expectations that make it feel like any resolution is beyond our abilities.

My brain naturally shifts to trying to *solve the whole problem*, to make it all *good* again. This is the particular talent of females, the curse of make-it-better-mommies. Trouble is, many of motherhood's—or even life's—challenges are too big for huge, instant solutions. The path out of most problems rarely comes to us in a single sitting.

Enter the baby step. Don't look to solve it all. Just search for a toehold to get you started in the right direction. A bit of *better* can be all you need when *good* isn't yet in view.

> Don't look to solve it all. Just search for a toehold to get you started in the right direction. A bit of better can be all you need when good isn't yet in view.

You need a start. A nudge. Something—anything—ideally something you can do within the hour.

The best baby steps have physical components, and they usually are associated with something positive. It's like the counselor who advised the woman to go take a walk. Often when you're stymied by fear, giving your body something to do will free your mind a bit to think. It's why cooking is sometimes one of the best baby steps. Kneading bread, for example, is physical, tactile, and concrete. Something wonderful comes out of the work of your hands. You've made something that was only tasteless ingredients before you started. The aroma alone sends a message of comfort. It accomplishes something comforting, and it occupies your mind.

I recently read that hospitals are giving knitting lessons and knitting supplies to chemo patients. As a knitter, this made loads of sense to me. Chemo demands lots of time just sitting, waiting to feel the nasty side effects of the medicine kick in. Lots of time for fear and stress to have a field day in your head. Knitting is a marvelous physical distraction because it's basic enough to still allow your mind lots of freedom. Also, it accomplishes something comforting: hand-knit mittens, cozy scarves, lush, fluffy sweaters. Doesn't it take your pulse rate down just thinking about it?

Making something from nothing gives us courage. Creating in the face of all that cellular destruction is one of the best baby steps around. Even if all you get done is one row, it's one row that wasn't there before. Again, it is concrete, positive, and tactile. These are powerful forces.

But what if you can't think of a blessed thing to make it better? There have been days when I've been so overcome with fear and worry that I just couldn't think. When I've been in such a dark place that bread-making and knitting are too weak to battle the panic. When you're in that awful, dark, frozen place, cry out with three little words: "Show me, Lord."

God truly is in the details—every last one of them. And he has promised over and over again to give us wisdom when we request it. Psalm 116 says, "The Lord is gracious and righteous; our God is full of compassion. The Lord protects the simplehearted; when I was in great need, he saved me" (vv. 5–6).

When I can't see the forest for the trees—be it for fear or anger—that's exactly how I feel: simplehearted. Not simpleminded—I know my brain is in there somewhere, but my weak and scared heart won't let it kick in. It is then that I ask God to show me the next step. And on the really bad days, I'll ask him to show me the smallest step I can handle. Because some days it feels like I can only move half an inch forward. You can trust God to send you half an inch if that's all you can handle. He will. It might comfort you to know that the next verse in that psalm reads, "Be at rest once more, O my soul, for the Lord has been good to you" (Ps. 116:7).

> I ask God to show me the next step. And on the really bad days, I'll ask him to show me the smallest step I can handle.

When you are frozen with fear or worry, find a soft, quiet place and sit for a moment. Or if you're somewhere you can't hide away for a moment (like the waiting room in the pediatrician's—or even the oncologist's—office), close your eyes and take a deep breath. Take a good, deep breath that fills up your lungs as you count to four or six; hold it for four counts; then exhale as you count to eight. If you do that four or five times, your body gets more oxygen and your muscles relax.

On a recent airplane flight, I read a stress-reducing exercise recommended by fitness expert Michael Sena.[11] He meant it for anxious airplane passengers, but I have used it many places, including the dreaded dentist's chair. Using deep breaths, count backwards from fifty, with an inhale for fifty, an exhale for forty-nine, an inhale for forty-eight, and so on. Do this until you get to twenty. Then do a full breath—inhale *and* exhale for nineteen, inhale and exhale for eighteen, etc., until you get all the way down to one. It will be chemically impossible for you to remain as stressed as you were when you started at fifty. The counting—I think especially because it is backwards—occupies just enough of your brainpower to stop the panic-born slide show of disastrous thoughts and allow you to concentrate on your breathing.

As you breathe, ask God—in words or what the Bible refers to as "groans of the spirit"—to show you a baby step, a toehold, a shred of what you need to send you away from the anxiety and toward the solution. Ask him for something you can do within the next hour if not right this minute. He'll know exactly what to send you.

> Ask God for something you can do within the next hour if not right this minute. He'll know exactly what to send you.

The story of Hagar from Genesis 21 offers a prime example of this. Hagar had been employed as the world's first surrogate mother, so to speak. Abraham, her master, was growing impatient with the Lord's promise to send him offspring. Abraham's wife, Sarah, who had been barren for decades, decided to take the matter of their descendents into her own hands. She had Abraham sleep with their servant Hagar, who subsequently bore him a son. When God fulfilled his promise and sent Abraham a son through Sarah, poor Hagar and her son, Ishmael, were demoted to third wheel mighty quick. In fact, she and her son were sent into the desert. Given some food, some water, and told to hit the road and never come back.

As you can imagine, it didn't take long for the food and water to run out. In one of the most sad and desperate scenes of the Old Testament, Hagar laid her son in the only bit of shade she could find—under a bush—and then lay herself down to die. She even lay down "about a bowshot away" so she couldn't hear his dying cries. (What mother could stand that?)

Hagar was paralyzed with a fear that had sunk right into despair. Every mother has been there, when things looked so bad you just wanted to lay down and never be heard from again. There in the middle of the arid, blazing hot desert, there seem to be no baby steps to be found.

Ah, but God heard Ishmael's cries. He called to Hagar. Genesis 21:19 says, "Then God opened her eyes and she saw a well of water. So she went and filled the skin with water and gave the boy a drink." I'm fascinated by the fact that it does not say, "God made a well appear," but that "God opened her eyes." If God can be trusted to show Hagar a well in a decidedly life-and-death situation, can we not trust him to open our eyes to the baby step that might be right in front of us in our own distress?

Hagar didn't even ask God for help. How much more will our heavenly Father give us if we ask? Remember that flag from my September 11 walk? That was an answer to prayer. And—here's the important point to remember—it was an answer *I could have never come up with on my own.* You can trust God to give you the foothold you need, and it will be the very best one for your state of mind at that moment. It may be an object, an idea, a phone call, or the knowledge of whom to call. It may be a song or a verse or one small act.

Do it. No matter how nonsensical it seems—for as I've said, baking bread and planting flags heal even if they make no sense. After you've done it, and you feel that foothold, take a moment to really feel it. On the high wire, once you've taken a step you need to use your limbs to balance yourself a bit before you take a next step. Rushing ahead will more than likely throw off the balance you've gained with the last step. Let your baby step do its job—steadying you. Then, when you can feel its benefits, pray for the next baby step. And go on.

Fear-Facing Questions

Where are you trying to make it all *good?* Can you refocus your attention to just making the current situation *better?* What are the small steps available to you today?

Fear Fighter

Using deep breaths, count backwards from fifty, with an inhale for fifty, an exhale for forty-nine, an inhale for forty-eight, and so on. Do this until you get to twenty. Then do a full breath—inhale *and* exhale for nineteen, inhale and exhale for eighteen, etc., until you get all the way down to one. It will be chemically impossible for you to remain as stressed as you were when you started at fifty.

Faith-Finding Verse

The Lord is gracious and righteous; our God is full of compassion. The Lord protects the simplehearted; when I was in great need, he saved me. Be at rest once more, O my soul, for the Lord has been good to you.
Psalm 116:5–7

Challenge 2:
We Can Weaken Fear with Preparation
Life Skills at the Shopping Mall? You Betcha.

It's tough raising a middle-schooler these days. They need independence, yet they seem like walking targets for the dark side of this world. They're almost old enough to do so many things—but the *almost* is such a big, gray, debatable sea of doubt and fear.

It is hard to cling to the belief that my eleven-year-old daughter needs to learn to do things on her own. Life is already so hard at that age—I just hate to think of some avoidable difficulty making things worse. Yet she must learn from her own mistakes and learn not to rely on me to save the day (as I am so wont to do!).

Mandy is cautious by nature, and I would be doing her a disservice by not actively helping her overcome any undue caution in appropriate ways. She needs to learn to stand up for herself in a tight spot, to find solutions to thorny problems, and be her own person. All good, vital growth, and all maturation *will not happen without risk.* Simply put, I should be nudging my little chick out of the nest or she will never learn to fly.

Now no good mother eagle is going to whack her baby out of the nest and offer her up as prey to the greedy forces of gravity. It has to happen in small steps. Nudges. Which lands us at the mall.

Allow me to explain. Any parent of a young girl faces the eventual decision of when to let her go to the mall alone. The mall. You know, that place where it seems like 90 percent of all abductions take place? In fact that's far from true, but for me the mall looms like a bastion of nasty people waiting to do something to my precious daughter. Again, if I were to look at the actual probability of something happening to Mandy at the mall, it would be small. But you can't convince my emotions of that.

And my daughter isn't interested in hearing any of it. For as you and I both know, hanging out at the mall is one of the rituals of middle-school life. It's the social epicenter, whether we like it or not. And, truth be told, I do consider it slightly more contained and secure than just walking around downtown.

Now don't melt your Mars bars. I don't let my eleven-year-old daughter go to the mall alone. Not *yet*.

It has occurred to me, though, that this right of socialization is on my daughter's sixth- or seventh-grade horizon. It has also occurred to me that this is mighty deep water just to dive into. I want her to wade in, slowly. *Nudges* are needed. I want her—and me—to get used to the idea of going somewhere unsupervised and all that's involved in that level of independence. So, even when she was only ten, I started thinking about those nudges.

> If I were to look at the actual probability of something happening to Mandy at the mall, it would be small. But you can't convince my emotions of that.

The prelude, oddly enough, was to hear her camp stories. The more I asked about what went on at summer camp, the more I heard stories of good judgment, independent thought, and even wrong choices that she now knew were wrong. I'll admit, that step was more for me than her. I needed to bolster my confidence in her judgment. Much like our sleepover issue from an earlier chapter, I think it helped her to know I was gaining confidence in her ability to handle herself.

Then I had to think of a good training program. Yes, *think*. Deliberately plot out how we were going to get from complete-Mom-supervision to complete-Momless-independence. The key point here is that it was not a one-step program. This was a long-term operation—and it's not in its final stages even though Mandy is now eleven. It really doesn't matter that this is about the mall either. It can be about any stage of independence—any necessary risk for our children that breeds fear for us. Bicycling to the library, walking to a friend's house, crossing the street, going to college, staying home alone—they're all the same. These kinds of risks are best taken in stages and *before* they jump up on us.

It's all too easy, I've found, to wait until a given request has come to you, make the one-step decision that your child is ready to do something, and then turn into a ball of fear while it takes place. If we can take a moment to predict what growth steps our kids will face soon and start engineering some nudges to prepare them, then everyone's better off.

I'll tell you how we handled (and are still handling) the mall scenario—in all its nudges—so you can get an idea of what I'm talking about. Then take a moment to think about what's facing your kids (and freaking their mother) in their near future and see if the same tactics might apply.

The first step was thinking about what skills are needed to wander the mall alone. One of the basic ones was making sure Amanda knew how to be at a given point at a given time. That, for us, meant something so basic as buying a watch. I never even thought about it—Mandy knew how to tell time, but because she'd never been anywhere alone, she didn't own a watch yet. Talk about a baby step. But if I hadn't been actively looking at the situation, I don't think I'd have even identified the need.

It served as a good discussion point. As we shopped for a watch, we talked about how I'd need to know she could identify a meeting point, figure out how much time it takes to get there from where she was, and find her way there. And so, over the watch counter at JC Penney, my daughter's independence training began.

Step two was to wander the mall and pick a few good meeting places. I let her show me she knew were the Dairy Queen counter was if she was standing in front of McDonald's.

Step three was to let her shop in a small store by herself for ten minutes—with me, of course, standing just outside the one and only entrance/exit, trying to look calm and natural as my fingernails were digging into my Starbucks paper cup. It was a test. We'd set it up that way. Her challenge was to spend her ten minutes any way she wanted but to make good and sure she was standing right in front of me at the store's entrance when those ten minutes were up. I'll admit it was a goofy, extreme example, but I think that's what made it acceptable—for both of us. Mandy passed with flying colors.

Step four involved a longer time unsupervised but with a buddy. I am not prepared—and am not sure I'll ever be willing—to let Mandy wander the mall *all* alone. The buddy system you remember from swimming lessons at summer camp is the cardinal rule here. Never go alone. With ten-year-old girls, who seem to naturally travel in packs anyway, that was not much of an issue. Now give it a few years, throw a few boys into the mix, and I'm sure it won't be so easy.

Mandy and her friend had one hour to wander the mall together and meet me back at a predetermined location. I had called the mother of the friend, explained what I was doing (she rather liked the idea, for her daughter needed a little independence training too), and we set a date. I stayed at the mall for that hour as well, trying as best I could not to tail them. And oh boy, was that hard.

I admit, I ended up at a nail salon getting a manicure because the salon had a huge glass storefront that looked out into the main section of the mall. Manicure espionage. Only a mother could dream that up, don't you think? By the way, this is one situation in which I think those nifty two-mile walkie-talkies you can get now would have been a big bonus. Sure, I wouldn't have expected her to call me, but just knowing she could reach me would have been a real comfort. We own a pair now.

Mandy and her friend both knew, in no uncertain terms, that failure to show up on time at the designated meeting point would be total failure. I did not allow them to be even two minutes late (ah, digital watches). It was a test. Failing it would mean we could not graduate to the next step. They knew that. The level of importance we placed on the girls' conduct communicated to them, I hope, the burden of responsibility that goes along with increased independence. We discussed, in advance, what to do in several eventualities—if they were stuck somewhere like waiting in a line to buy something, if they got separated, if someone approached them, etc. In essence, we gave them the skills they needed to handle the situation. They exceeded my expectations.

The next steps increased the time allowed, but always with a friend and always with me in the mall somewhere. I still have to think about what issue will convince me that she is ready to have me off the premises, but we have some time. And truth be told, it is not hard to kill a couple of hours at the mall and stay out of kid-sight. So everybody wins. And I feel good that my daughter is learning, in small safe steps, to be alone.

Why go to all this trouble? Because—and I think this is worth saying—*it is good for her to be alone.* It is important that I deliberately move her towards being independent of me. That is my job as a parent. Yes, I'm raising her, but I prefer to think of it as *launching* her. My job is to meet and conquer the fear involved in setting her free as a healthy adult. I must also meet and conquer my own fear that harm will come to her. Because, scary as it is to admit, harm will come to her. At some point sooner or later, bad things will come to her. My job is to do my best to see that they don't *overcome* her. And for me, baby steps are the path to that goal.

All this sounds like a lot of work and a hefty load of planning—hard and thoughtful planning. When you are busy unloading the dishwasher or driving to the week's twelfth soccer practice, the prospect of scanning your daughter's social horizon seems impossible. How do we get to this level of sensitivity, of proactive rather than reactive parenting? How do we fight the fears we can't even see clearly yet?

> Yes, I'm raising her, but I prefer to think of it as launching her. My job is to meet and conquer the fear involved in setting her free as a healthy adult.

The answer does not lie in twentieth-century technology, psychology, or physiology. It lies in the centuries-old process of writing. One of your best parenting tools—especially for the fear-fighting parts of parenting—is pen and paper.

When planning, analyzing, or facing a really thorny problem, writing it down is always an excellent step. My eyes popped when I read the following in Susan Shaughnessy's marvelous book for writers entitled *Walking on Alligators*: "A writer without a journal is like a high-wire artist working without a net."[12] I just love it when God sends neon signs down from heaven. Writer or not, anything that serves as a high-wire artist's net is worth our attention. I'd revise it, for our purposes, to read, "A mom without a journal is like a high-wire artist working without a net." Especially for us moms, it was a different sentence from that page that struck the point home: "A writer uses a journal to try out the new step in front of the mirror."

Moms use a journal to try out the new step, the new stage, the new nudge, in front of the mirror. To take the colossal long-term endeavor that is parenting and dissect it into bite-sized chunks of here and now. To find the nudges that will get us and our babies from nest to flight. Even if you haven't a single cell of literary aspiration in your body, a journal is a safe place to let it all hang out. I have often found that the act of writing out a problem in all its gory detail, with every conceivable repercussion and consequence, restores my control of it. Paper is a safe place to look the terror—or even just the complexity—in the face. Somehow my brain knows that if I can contain it on paper, the problem isn't completely beyond my ability to deal with it.

> *Moms use a journal to try out the new step, the new stage, the new nudge, in front of the mirror.*

A journal is a magical place. In there, I can test out things I can do to help me cope. I can open the emotional safety valve and indulge in a bit of worst-case scenario building, or I can simply let the emotions all come out so they don't fester inside. I can privately try on an emotion or solution I'm not yet ready to fully embrace. It is a place for me to play around with plans and ideas on how to get from where I am to where I want to be.

Some of the best nudges have come to me off the pages of my journals. There are days when it feels as though I am taking dictation from God, and the clear steps come leaping off the page. Then there are days when I am simply allowing myself to think thoughts and get them out of the way. There are lists, charts, pages of pure drivel, questions circled, and arrows pointing from one paragraph to another four pages over. There are pages that are crystal clear, brimming with great solutions, and pages that only seem to muddy the waters. I think those muddy pages are just as important as the clear ones because *every* stage of the process contributes to our success.

The freedom of a journal's privacy opens up places that sometimes just need airing. Otherwise those thoughts and fears could hang around and get in the way of more important decisions. My engagement journals are a prime example. We've been renovating our house this summer, and in all the packing and unpacking I uncovered my journals from when I became engaged to my husband, Jeff. There, in page after page, were the fears of a twenty-six-year-old woman about to commit her life to one man. Forever.

There were the gushy romantic plans and the excitement of being madly in love. But there were also pages covered with concerns and questions. They were good fears, valid fears, ones that were worth exploring. Was I sure about this relationship? How could I know—for sure—that he was "the one"? People change so much as they age—would we have what it took to last? What if there were secrets about him I didn't know? What if I got very sick, or he got very sick, or something drastic like that? I knew I loved him, that we were compatible, but there was still so much I didn't know.

I *couldn't* know. I haven't met anyone who knew for absolute certain. You just don't get to. Getting married is an act of faith. My pastor told me at the time that anyone who isn't good and scared at the prospect of marriage hasn't really looked at what they're doing. In other words, he told me the fear was a sign that I was undertaking this sacrament with the healthy dose of apprehension it deserved.

Being able to write out all those worries helped me hold those fears without letting them hold me. Denying they were there wouldn't have been healthy. At the same time, talking about them at length might have given them more attention than they deserved. Sure, if they refused to subside and became very heavy concerns, that would be a signal

> *Being able to write out all those worries helped me hold those fears without letting them hold me.*

to me that they did deserve more attention. But they were not. They were the underlying, healthy, take-this-thing-seriously kind of concerns that every prenuptial woman ought to have. By admitting they were there, committing them to the finite nature of paper where I could hold them up and examine their merits, I could see them in the proper perspective. Had I completely ignored them, shooed them away as the emotional equivalent of a gnat, they might have picked away at my confidence. No, to write them, to take them out and look at sometimes but then to put back in the drawer, *that* was the best place for them. Those journals were a place where each page was its own baby step.

We can run from fear, but in many cases it's far healthier to *walk* away from it. Step by step. The power of the nudge harnesses whatever tiny increments your soul and courage will allow. The magic is that even the smallest of steps removes you a bit further away from the fear. Then, bit by bit or page by page, you may find yourself far enough away from a fear to *really* see it with perspective and without the distortion of panic. Then—and only then—can you act wisely.

You most often find from that distant vantage point that it is not nearly as bad as it seemed from up close. Such knowledge is the powerful seed of courage.

Fear-Facing Questions

Where do you need to start thinking about launching your little ones? What's on your children's horizon that you can begin to prepare them to face? Remember that stepping out of their (and your) comfort zone is an important part of growing up.

Fear Fighter

Start keeping a journal. Give yourself the private time and place to work it all out on paper. Even ten minutes a day can help you sort through a thorny problem or plan a complex solution.

Faith-Finding Verse

If the Lord delights in a man's way, he makes his steps firm; though he stumble, he will not fall, for the Lord upholds him with his hand.

Psalm 37:23–24

Challenge 3:
We Can Fake Out Our Fear

The Magical Fear-Fighting Pajamas and Other Unlikely Tools

We spent this chapter talking about the power of nudges and baby steps. We learned that some of the best first baby steps are illogical ones. Now I want to look at some of the more unlikely first steps that may be the most potent footholds of all. The unlikely ones—the downright silly ones—are ideally suited for very big fears. It almost *needs* to be slightly absurd to work against the really big stuff, I think.

Silly or not, the best baby steps need to feel like action. Even if it's just yelling. Let me share an example with you.

When I was little, I had an irrational, bone-deep fear of sirens. No matter where I was, the sound of a siren would send me into a panic. In many ways, it still does a bit. Sirens mean something, somewhere near enough for me to hear, has gone wrong. Very wrong. Something has created the need for firefighters, policemen, or paramedics. Big trouble.

I think this is a common fear for children. It's a highly distinctive sound immediately associated with stuff that can't be good. Until you turn it on its ear.

Sometime in my life—and I honestly don't recall when or who—someone taught me to reclassify that sound. Sirens don't mean trouble. They mean *help is on the way*. If you're caught in a burning building, that siren sound means your help is coming up the driveway to get you out of there. If your loved one is on the floor unconscious, sirens mean paramedics are about to burst through the door and give him the immediate care he needs.

Wow. I had never thought of it that way. Suddenly, that person had handed me the keys to focus my attention not on the problem but on the *solution* that was in progress.

> Sirens don't mean trouble. They mean help is on the way.

It's not just the shift in thinking, however, that holds the magic in this for me. It's the magic of an action-oriented baby step. I needed to find a way to take this new idea and put it on its feet—to get it out of the realm of intangible thought and give me some small action to jump-start my courage. I needed to yell.

Now, whenever I hear a siren when I'm with my children, we all call out, "Help is on the way!" The more the panic, the louder the yell—often we are as loud as the siren's wail, if not louder. And it works.

I was delighted to hand down to my children this instant antidote. Their fear of sirens lasted about two days. A couple of doses of "Help is on the way!" and it was gone, all because of the baby step of an exclamation. My young niece was afraid of a strong wind one afternoon, and I gave her a yell of her own to face it down. It worked just as well.

Sometimes, though, it isn't about action at all but about sensation. Sensations are highly potent baby steps. Why? Because sensations are like a logic-free hotline to our physiology. They are a fast way to our psyche because they can sidestep conscious thought.

That's why I'm here to tell you that one of the most powerful baby steps of all is right beside you, in your own bureau. Pajamas.

Yes, you heard me. PJ's can fight fear.

Now I know you're thinking, "I was willing to go along with the bread-baking thing, even though it was a bit of a stretch, but now that Allie woman has gone too far." Stay with me for a moment, because these are some of the best fear-fighting tactics I know.

First, I think pajamas work *because* the concept is so preposterous. It's a bit absurd, which is a close cousin to funny. Pajamas are warmth, comfort, rest. I can't think of any stressful situation I associate with pajamas. They're soft, cuddly, and endearing. Your body knows them instantly. Putting on your pajamas harnesses the power of physical sensation to bring down your heart rate. It doesn't matter if your brain doesn't buy into the idea; your subconscious knows exactly how to process that sensation.

Try it some day, even if it's lunchtime. When you are stressed out about something and you can't think clearly, go put on your pajamas for an hour and see what happens. It works. Really. It doesn't surprise me at all that pajamas have come into fashion. We need them. We crave what they represent on the most basic of levels.

Those silly things like yells and pajamas work because they are a kinesthetic memory—a body-borne impulse derived straight from our senses. A basic input that gets to bypass our logical brain so it goes straight to our physiological state. It's what makes a hug a *hug*. It's what makes a blanket a *blankie*.

> *Try it some day, even if it's lunchtime. When you are stressed out about something and you can't think clearly, go put on your pajamas for an hour and see what happens.*

No mother will minimize the power of "loveys." Any one of us who has tried to wean a little one off his or her blankie knows the power of those grungy, frayed scraps of fabric. Adults are more sophisticated; we like to think we're above the blankie mentality—but sometimes that gets in the way. When you are stressed, scared, and can't think clearly, it pays to tap into this sensory powerhouse. It may not be a solution in itself, but it can somehow take enough of the edge off a situation to allow your brain a chance to work. Then, you may find that first *better* step.

If not PJ's, then maybe it is a different sense element. My dad was a real estate broker, and long before the advent of aromatherapy, he knew the physiological power of scent. He used to put drops of vanilla extract on the light bulbs of a house on the market. Why? Because it smells like baking cookies. What's more homey than that?

Baking. Knitting. Comfy socks. The sound of the waterfall on your back deck. The warmth and aroma of a cup of hot tea. Your husband's favorite sweatshirt. The Brandenburg Concertos. A red clown nose. Go with your first impulse and don't edit your thinking. As far as I'm concerned, the less logical it is, the more powerful it is. Whatever it is, you'll know it in a heartbeat. When you find it, stop telling yourself it's silly or superfluous and wield that powerful tool to your advantage.

One of my favorite parental examples of this came from my days as a working mother. The daily separation ritual that working mothers dread is really no different than the separation anxiety that is the universal curse of mothers. There are days where we and our children happily wave goodbye and trot off to our separate adventures of school and grocery shopping. Then there are days when it feels as one wise mother put it, "We are wrenching our hearts out from inside our chests to let them walk around outside our bodies."

I read somewhere about a mother's ritual of planting a kiss on her daughter's open palm. It is a tender act in itself, but it is the power of the sense memory that fascinated me. This mother wore a particular color lipstick every day. When she said goodbye, this mother planted not just a physical kiss, but a visual lipstick kiss in her preschooler's palm. In other words, a kiss her daughter could not only feel and remember but *see* for a while. It seems to me, the more senses you can involve, the more powerful force you have. Whenever this little girl felt scared or alone, she could look at her palm, see the evidence of her mother right there in the palm of her hand, and squeeze her chubby hand around it in a long-distance kiss and hug. I adopted the idea with great success any time my little children and I were to be separated for a while.

Grown-ups need sensation-based comfort too. When my mother died, I had the irrational craving to wear her jewelry. The minute I got my hands on certain items, I put them on. Not because I was itching to get at her diamonds, but because the gems had been *hers*. The funeral home director gave me the rings she had on her fingers when she died, and I have not taken them off since. Not because they are physically beautiful—although they are—but because they touched her skin. Because they *fit*, and that gives me a deep, inexplicable sense of continuity. The particular jingle of her bracelets is like no other sound in the universe, and when I hear them, she is somehow with me. That is a sense memory. I thought it odd and silly at first, but I have come to recognize and value the comfort I get from those sensations.

Your favorite sweater of your husband's isn't just about color or shape—it's about how he has stretched out the cuffs, how it smells just a bit like him, what it feels like against your cheek when you snuggle up against him—all sense memories. Blankies aren't about what they *are*, they're mostly about *where they've been*. That's why our little darlings are so loathe to let us wash their blankies—they may be germs to us, but they're sense memories to our children.

Harness that power. Is there a physical object you can share with your children during a stressful time? I have often given my children a shirt, scarf, or some other object of mine to sleep with if they are worried or I am far away.

The pajamas I wore in the hospital with CJ are tattered and thin, but they are enormously comforting to me. I'll never trash them. I love the idea of making a quilt from significant pieces of clothing in your life—the shirt you wore when you met your husband, your son's first soccer jersey, a baby blanket, that scarf you bought on vacation in New Hampshire.

It is wise to allow your senses to do what logic often cannot: bring calm. Use them.

Fear-Facing Questions

What sense memories bring you peace? What favorite objects of clothing bring you comfort? How could you use your senses to bring peace into a stressful situation?

Fear Fighter

When you're stumped, slip into your pajamas. Put on your favorite jammies, your cushiest slippers, your coziest robe, and then see if the problem doesn't seem just a bit less fearful.

Faith-Finding Verse

The Lord is my shepherd, I shall not be in want. He makes me lie down in green pastures, he leads me beside quiet waters, he restores my soul.

Psalm 23:1–3

The Nudge Factor

The concept of stepping away from fear in small increments isn't as comfortable as we'd like. Most of us would rather set off and solve the problem in a single bound. Things rarely solve themselves that easily. More often than not, life solves itself in nudges.

Nudges of growth are the very core of parenting. Children grow in nudges. They learn in nudges. They become adults in baby steps. Good parenting is breaking life down into bite-sized chunks.

It is wise to remember that if growth does indeed come bit by bit, then courage comes in nudges as well. In the age of the Quick-Fix-Everything, it is easy to assume that with just the right strategy, we'll all be fine and fearless tomorrow. Peace is just a diet, self-help book, or retreat away. Very few things in life work that way, which is why patience is a virtue.

> In the age of the Quick–Fix–Everything, it is easy to assume that with just the right strategy, we'll all be fine and fearless tomorrow. Very few things in life work that way, which is why patience is a virtue.

I assumed it would take me four or five lessons to get me across the low wire. It took months. I wanted to take the learning in hour-long lessons, but my teacher was wise enough to realize I couldn't handle more than a half-hour lesson for the first few times. He was right; after even twenty-five minutes my mind and body were taxed to their limit.

In my lessons, I fell a lot. Then I'd get all tense and doubt the wisdom of my being there in the first place and fall more. Things changed when my teacher started engaging me in conversation as I stepped on the wire. He'd ask me about the book, my kids, anything to keep me talking. Then he encouraged me to simply chatter to him while I was on the wire. He handed me, in essence, a tool— a way to end run my overanalytical brain and let my body do the job at hand. Forcing me to think about two things at once kept me from obsessing about the fact that I might fall. Instead I'd be thinking about our conversation and just start walking. The time I crossed the wire most easily was when, on his urging, I just "up and did it." Stuck my foot out, found the wire, and then kept stepping. Not that I could have done it without all the training, but success came when I stopped thinking the thing through so much and just kept going.

God did not part the Jordan River to let the Israelites through *until they put their feet in the water*. Mary had to say "yes" first before the Holy Spirit filled her and she became the mother of Jesus. Recognize that God may be asking you to take the first step in faith, to find the baby step and start the process, before he sends you the grace and guidance you'll need to finish the job. As I said, he didn't send Hagar the well, he just opened her eyes to see it. She had to go fetch a drink with her own hands. And he didn't start with a full course meal and a ticket home; he started with a simple drink of water.

You may think the concept of donning PJ's instead of carefully analyzing your fears is sugarcoating the issue. It isn't. Considering the possibility that we need to end run around our brain implies that we can't just *will* our way out of any given fear. Not everything in life is just "mind over matter." Capitalizing on sensations to reduce our fear is neither trickery nor façade. It is accessing every available resource to meet a goal. It is giving your brain all the clearance it can have to work through a thorny problem.

The bottom line in all of this is that what matters most is to keep moving, to deny fear's capacity to freeze us. It does not matter if you must step away from your fear—or nudge your little ones to courage—in the tiniest of increments. Forward is forward is forward. A small step is no less a step than a big step.

You are on the way. And that is what matters.

Chapter 7

THE STUMBLE

*"I'm always afraid I will forget a child somewhere.
You hear about it happening. I know it's unlikely,
but I'm still afraid of it."*

*"I fear I won't 'hear' God's directions for raising my children,
and I will fail in raising them the way he wants me to."*

"I fear I'll forget to play tooth fairy—again!"

*"I'm afraid that my children will hate me and remember
terrible things I've said and done. I fear that no matter how
I do things, there will be something that ruined them."*

What Happens When We Fall?

I have a recurring, awful vision of my daughter Mandy when she is in her twenties. I can picture it in excruciating detail because I've been there. She's sitting in a coffee bar (it will be biologically impossible, I assure you, for this child not to love coffee) with a female friend, and they'll be telling stories. Not just any stories, but the kind of stories I used to call "Etta stories." Etta was my mother.

It is one of the bonding practices of female adulthood to get together and play an emotional version of "Can you top this?" We relate horrible, imperfect, issue-creating, badly thought out, or just plain embarrassing things our mothers have done for us or to us.

My mother had character in heroic proportions—in the very best and sometimes the worst sense of the word. And man oh man, she used to drive me nuts. We saw the world quite differently. We loved each other, but we were oil and water in many respects. So Etta stories abounded. As will— *gasp*—Allie stories.

I am just as much a character—if not . . . um . . . more so—than my mother. And I can just see twenty-seven-year-old Amanda at a coffee bar (it is much more comforting to picture her there than on a therapist's couch), rolling her eyes over a mocha latte, groaning, hand on her forehead, recapping my latest error for her friends.

I know down to my toes that this is a 100 percent accurate prediction. There *will* be Allie stories. If I'm lucky, they may not be the kind that show up on *Jerry Springer*. But rest assured, there will be stories. You know what? There already *are* stories.

We're going to mess up as mothers. Assuredly. Repeatedly. We are imperfect, emotion-laden, reason-abandoning, hormone-crazed, sleep-deprived bundles of humanity, and we're going to make mistakes.

Mothers have a huge capacity to obsess about this. I can't tell you how many moms cite "ruining my kids" or "not being the mother my kids deserve" as one of their top parenting fears. We want the best for our kids, and we easily convince ourselves that we might not be able to achieve it. We're fabulous at cataloguing our shortcomings. We want to be the perfect mom for our kids but are painfully aware that it seems beyond our reach.

On a basic level, we're correct—we cannot be perfect mothers. The certainty of our imperfection is one of parenting's essential truths. There is no *if* in the picture, it's all about *when* we will fail. Count on it; we will fail—frequently—as parents.

This bugs us because we know the stakes of parenting. Some of us are still carrying the battle scars of bad parenting we had as children. We instinctively know the potential for harm, and we fear our capacity to inflict it.

Not only that, but we all want our kids to love us. We want them to think of us as fine, loving parents, to admire us now and speak well of us when we've gone. We want that to happen for us, but we know how we feel about our own parents and that "bad" is in the mix as often as (if not more so than) "good."

Our children will not approve, enjoy, or benefit from everything we do. We will hamper their growth and development. We'll embarrass them. We will wound them.

> Some of us are still carrying the battle scars of bad parenting we had as children. We instinctively know the potential for harm, and we fear our capacity to inflict it.

If you had any delusions of spectacular parenting, any delusions of staying flawlessly up here on the high wire, now would be a good time to toss them out. There is no such thing. All we can hope for is to do the best parenting job we can in the time that we have, in our current emotional state, and with the at-best incomplete information we have.

Which means falling is absolutely, positively, undeniably part of the picture.

Make no mistake: gravity wins.

If we do it right, though, gravity only wins the battle.

Love wins the war.

Challenge 1:
We Fear Our Children Will Hate Us for Our Mistakes

Mom's Gargantuan Blowup over Beating Traffic for Fun

Our parenting is going to include gargantuan errors. I remember the one time I screamed at my children. "One time"? Ha! Who am I kidding?

Ahem. I am reminded of the *worst time* I screamed at my children. I mean *really* screamed. Tearstained, door-slamming, object-throwing (not at them, mind you), end-of-my-rope screaming. What's worse, I'm embarrassed to say that it was not over anything I now consider major. Isn't that always the way it is? The really big blowups—because they are most often the last straw in a long list of frustrations—often are not about the really big issues. For me—and I'm cringing as I type this—it was about getting the car loaded to go away for the weekend. One of those "we have to get out of here early so we can beat the traffic" scenarios.

Beating the traffic. Still worse, I was thinking about beating the traffic so the kids could have a chance to swim in the hotel pool that evening. So it was *beating the traffic for fun.* I raged to the point of bringing my children to tears over *fun.*

To borrow one of my daughter's favorite phrases, "How lame is that?" How could that possibly be something worth one of my worst parental blunders?

Beats me.

Most of us can be good parents when things go right; it's how we parent when things go wrong that tests our mettle.

It's also how our kids develop their own mettle. Just as Eleanor Roosevelt said, "A woman is like a tea bag. You never know how strong she really is until she gets in hot water."

The truth is that we'll spend a lot of time in that hot water as parents. As a matter of fact, clinical psychologist and mother Dr. Paulette Toburen, the final member of our expert panel, explained to me that we *need* to make mistakes. Children need imperfect parents.

What?

Yes, it's true. Our children need us to be imperfect parents.

> Children need imperfect parents. What? Yes, it's true. Our children need us to be imperfect parents.

Renowned child development theorist D. W. Winnicott spent years studying what he called "the value of imperfect parenting."[13] He discovered that parental mistakes are actually fertile ground for learning. Our children need to experience what Winnicott called *empathic failures*. This means they learn to deal with failure and mistakes by watching us. When we mess up or fail to meet one of our children's needs, a vital learning process takes place: They learn to compensate and meet their own needs. If we meet all our children's needs all the time, they will develop no coping strategies of their own. We must fail them from time to time so they learn to be strong themselves.

Wow. That blew me away. My kids need my mistakes. And here I spend so much time fretting over my mistakes. Dr. Toburen advises us to avoid "the dangerous illusion of the perfect parent" and seek instead to be the "good enough parent who loves" and who teaches them, by example, that it is okay to make mistakes. She boiled Winnicott's theory down to marvelously human terms: "If Mom can make a mistake and live through it, so can I."

My kids remember Mom's gargantuan blowup over beating traffic for fun. I'll not gild the lily; this episode made a lasting, bad impression on them. Winnicott would have had a field day with the list of ways I failed to meet their needs. I asked them about it this morning, just to test my theory, and they could recall the day in ugly, regrettable detail.

I had messed up big time. I knew it. Even they knew it. Chances are, the way I was carrying on out in the driveway, the whole neighborhood knew it as well.

But—and here's the key—*it's not the only thing my children remember about it.* They remember that after I exploded, I went inside, sat down, and cried. Then I came to them and asked them to forgive me. Yes, they weren't listening to me well, and they were dawdling in that highly frustrating way in which kids are experts, but in no way did my punishment of them fit their minor crimes.

What we needed was to push past the anger and claw our way to forgiveness. Actually, the clawing was mostly on my part, for their instant, total forgiveness came in a heartbeat. There I was, down on the floor at their level, holding my arms out because I needed a king-size hug. They rushed to me because they needed to see the Mom they knew was somewhere beneath all that yelling. I knew my rage had scared them. They knew their behavior had put Mom over the edge. The only thing that was going to haul us out of that abyss was a dousing of forgiveness. It was a tender, raw moment that still today brings tears to my eyes.

The great blessing of children is that they can see us ripped bare, see every imperfection, and love us warts and all. There on that living room floor, we all learned what it means to love. I can never remove the bad of that afternoon, but I have added the powerful antidote of human kindness to that memory. In the words of writer Susan Shaughnessy, "We will make [mistakes]. Some of them will haunt us. But we must let them *haunt,* not *hinder*" (emphasis added).[14]

> The great blessing of children is that they can see us ripped bare, see every imperfection, and love us warts and all.

I did fail, and they did learn through it. Winnicott was right. This and many of the most valuable parenting experiences I have had involve getting back up again from a spectacular stumble—either mine or my child's. Such raw moments seem to be where the real lessons happen—not in the warm and fuzzy moments.

Moms shaking in your sneakers everywhere, listen to me: That will not be the last time I fail my children. Human parents *will* fail their children. On this high wire of parenting, we will always fall. But there is love, and that means there is hope.

Even if we fall badly—even really, really badly—the grace of our Lord Jesus Christ is an infallible net. Even the things that "ruin our kids," which cannot be mended, the horrors we cannot erase or take back, the damage inflicted, are not beyond the grace of God. His promise, "I will repay you for the years the locusts have eaten" (Joel 2:25), is true. Even if your worst fears come to be realized, even if your relationship with your child is damaged beyond what you feel is repairable, even if such damage has come by your own hand, none of these things is beyond the healing power of God.

The grace of God is more powerful than your worst mistake. There is no situation that he cannot put to a good and powerful use. For such places are where God is God. And we *cannot* ruin our kids *because* God is God.

Think for a moment about what that means. There are three elements in every parenting situation: the parent, the child, and God. Even if I totally mess up as a parent, I still don't own even 51 percent of the stock in my child's outcome. I'm only one-third of the picture. I do not have the majority here. God can work with and within my child to rise him or her to a fine outcome despite the worst possible parenting. You may even know people whose lives attest to this truth. Successful men and women have risen above childhoods of abuse, abandonment, deceit, and a host of other parental harms. There's a very good chance, then, that my first-grader can survive my forgetting to pick him up from school. Even if it does feel like a travesty the day I did it.

Each one of us were raised by imperfect parents. Lots of us turned out okay, or very close to okay, because we have a Lord who specializes in making lemonade from lemons. When we are at our worst is when his strength has the most power. The real transformation of a heart, the true growth toward our heavenly nature, doesn't come in the Hallmark-card moments. It is a treasure earned at tremendous cost. It comes in the sticky, ugly, regrettable, so-hard-you-want-to-scream moments. The moments we're sure we've ruined everything.

But wait—who's to say what "ruining" is? We don't have—and never will have—the full picture. We don't know how any bad experience will be used in our children's lives.

Consider Moses. Talk about a life worthy of its own *Oprah* show. Abandoned by his own mother—even if it was with the best of intentions. Moses was deceived by the parents who raised him. Raised in a culture steeped in discrimination, racism, and slavery, the man was a convicted murderer. What would your opinion be if someone from that background came to you today? It's the stuff of supermarket tabloids, and surely not the pedigree and resume you'd expect for the deliverer of God's people. Sounds like a ruined guy.

Good thing it's not up to us, for we would never have been able to see that Moses was exactly the guy for the job. For heaven's sake, even Moses couldn't get his arms around the idea at first. The third and fourth chapters of Exodus tell us that Moses tried very hard to convince God there surely was someone *else* with a better skill set. God insisted he was the one. His past—scars and all—made him who he was, and *who God chose.*

Ah, but even holy recruitment doesn't guarantee smooth sailing. Moses had his own spectacular stumbles. If you read Exodus carefully, Moses did not mature into a deliverer with a crystal-clean record. His leadership of the tribes of Israel had some definite rough spots—some definite "imperfect parenting." If even Moses can mess things up and still end up delivering an entire nation with God's help, then wouldn't you agree we stand a chance with our children?

We do. Because we love our children. And because God is God.

Fear-Facing Questions

Do you have a "Mom's gargantuan blowup over beating traffic for fun" story? What do you remember about that time? What do your kids remember? What have been the lasting impressions?

Fear Fighter

Say it over and over. Paste it to your fridge. Tape it to your bathroom mirror. Tattoo it on your forehead:

> *I cannot ruin my child.*
> *I am only one-third of the picture.*
> *My child is who he or she is.*
> *And God is God.*
> *I cannot ruin my child.*

Faith-Finding Verse

> *And we know that in all things God works for the good of those who love him, who have been called according to his purpose.*
>
> *Romans 8:28*

Challenge 2:
We Fear Our Failures Will Scar Our Children
Surviving the Unrecoverable and Living to Tell the Tale

I have scoured my childhood memories to come up with what I consider to be the greatest stumble—the greatest failure, if you will—between my mother and me. In the process, I have come to realize how much this particular event has shaped my life. I can say now that much of that shaping has been for good. But it has been hard-won goodness.

When I was in high school, my father developed heart disease. There were many hospital visits, medications, and assorted medical traumas. My parents did an outstanding job of keeping things feeling ordinary for their kids, of shielding us from the stress and complications of a serious illness. In her desire to protect a rather emotional and volatile teenage daughter, my mother chose to keep from me—and nearly everyone else—the fact that Dad's illness was terminal. I cannot imagine the emotional strain of letting me go off to college and to my first professional theater job that summer—both far away from home— knowing those months would likely be Dad's last. It is a tribute to the strength of her will that she was able to keep most of our friends—and to a large extent even Dad himself—from the certainty of his disease's final outcome.

Dad died while I was away at college my sophomore year. It was a difficult time for everyone. But for me the most difficult thing was to learn, through an inadvertent slip-up months later, that Dad's early death was inevitable. It was a crushing blow for me to discover that Dad had been terminally ill. As I saw it—and still see it—both my father and I had been robbed of the chance to say goodbye. My mother, out of love, chose to protect me from the *dying* if she couldn't protect me from the death. She couldn't understand that I would much rather have looked the dying in the face if it meant the chance to really say goodbye. I would rather have cried with him over his impending death than cry over him and a tube-strewn, nearly lifeless body in the cardiac intensive care unit.

This is irreparable damage. There is no way to make it better. Those months are lost forever; that chance to say goodbye can never be regained. It drove a king-size wedge between my mother and me. The night we hashed it out remains one of the worst fights Mom and I ever had.

It has never gone away. But I tell you the story because I want you to know that *we got past it*. It took the distance of years, the effort of hard loving, the understanding of parenthood, and the boundless grace of God, but it happened. God has taken that episode and transformed it into a bone-deep craving for truth, a desire to stare life in the face, a strong aversion to secrets, a belief in the power of honesty, a value of courage in life's messy parts. These are a large part of who I am today. My mother's actions are only one small part of that experience and what it has become in my life.

Neither are my own actions the majority of that lesson. I did not behave lovingly in the months following that revelation. My personality probably made the situation with my mother worse, rather than helping me to the healing of our relationship.

Only God can turn things like that around. Parenting is more than a two-way street; it's a three-part harmony. The final outcome of our lives is dependent not just on the parent or on the child—both human and flawed—but primarily on God.

Flaws were everywhere when my mother and I were yelling at each other, furious at how each other had chosen to react, clashing our way to some kind of understanding. We were struggling to know *why* each of us did what we did, even if we didn't agree with the choice.

I have been at that dark place with my mother. I will be at some similar place some regrettable day over some horrible failure with my own daughter. Right there, in the middle of all that harm and heartbreak, how do we survive? How do we find the way to transform it into a deep life lesson rather than an uncrossable chasm?

Believe it or not, it's all in the knees.

> Parenting is more than a two-way street, it's a three-part harmony. The final outcome of our lives is dependent not just on the parent or on the child—both human and flawed—but primarily on God.

One of my most difficult high-wire lessons was trying to learn how to right myself when I tipped over. I had learned the walking skill, but that will only take you so far on the wire. Once you start to take more than a few steps, the human body invariably starts to tip over on that tiny cable. I needed to learn how to recover from a slip or stumble.

The formula for righting yourself on a tightrope is quite simple—the trouble comes in the fact that it's *totally counterintuitive*. In other words, what you need to be doing is the exact opposite of what your instincts tell you. When you tip too far over or stumble, you *want* to flail, to wave your arms and reach out to either side of you for handrails that simply aren't there. Emotionally, isn't that how many of us react when things get wobbly—reach all over the place; flap around a lot?

It's not what we need to be doing. On the tightrope, you need to bend your knees. In a danger situation, most wire-walkers will squat or sit down. Get down on one knee. From a physics standpoint, it makes sense—the lower you are, the lower your center of gravity, the easier to stay upright. If you're falling, get down low.

Try telling that to your knees. They don't want to bend; they want to *bail*. When you're only two feet off the ground, every bone in your body wants to step off the wire, to reach out for the person spotting you, or to bail off the wire onto that nice, cushy crash pad underneath you. All of which is counterproductive if not downright harmful.

You cannot progress on the high wire until you've mastered this impulse. It makes sense, because once you make the next progression to a wire ten feet off the ground (I doubt I'll make it there anytime soon), you *can't* just hop off. There is no one beside you to spot you, and there are no midair handrails. You've got to learn how to recover your balance *on the wire,* and in most instances that means doing an end run around your basic instincts.

Sound like parenting? You can't just hop off; parenting is the ultimate nonrefundable ticket. As I've said before, we don't get the two-foot-high training wire in parenting— our walk starts in the high stakes mode from day one. And those of us who've tried to solve a sticky problem in what I'll call "flailing mode" have learned it is a most ineffectual coping strategy. So we need to master the wirewalker's recovery strategy just as much as our aerial counterparts.

Have you figured out the power in the metaphor yet? Here's a hint: It's about the getting down. As in down on your knees.

As in *prayer.*

Prayer is the crisis tool of every parent. Prayers for wisdom, for patience, for the ability to make a wise choice when the information is not clear. For the spine to get up and do it all over again. For the grace to sit down and listen to your child's point of view when you'd rather scream so loud they can hear you in the next zip code. For the strength to love when it feels nearly impossible. For protection when your defiant child has gone off and done something exceedingly stupid and possibly dangerous. For even ten minutes of peace so you can make it through the rest of the afternoon.

Ah, but it's not only about getting down; it's about looking up. The physical struggle for me as I squat down to catch my balance on the wire is that it *only* works *if* you keep your head and chest up. If you give in to your body's natural propensity to curl over as you crouch down, you'll fall for sure.

Fighting that urge is a tough battle. This, for me, takes a sheer act of will. My lower back muscles ached after the lesson because I had to fight so hard not to crouch over when I squatted down. I had to literally push my upper body up, straining one muscle against another to fight the involuntary response of curling over.

"I will lift mine eyes unto the hills, from whence cometh my help" (Psalm 121:1 KJV). When in trouble, when stumbling—either on the wire or in parenting—bend your knees and look up.

Folks, that's the living metaphor for prayer. It's a lesson every mother can use. The battles of parenting, like the challenges of wirewalking, are best met on your knees. And if you're like me, that takes a sheer act of will to counteract the impulse to curl in on myself. I'm instantly focusing on how bad the problem is, how I've messed up, how much damage has been done. Does that help matters? Not a bit. I could do myself much more good by focusing on what a mighty God I have. If I've got a whopping battle, I'd better be recognizing what a whopping God I've got to fight it. I love one of author Julie Barnhill's favorite phrases, "This is a God-sized problem," because it's a turn of phrase that fights like my muscles against the impulses. Have you ever stopped to consider that we can affect more solutions to problems in thirty minutes of prayer than in ten hours of scheming and brain-racking? I don't know about you, but if given the choice between racking my brains or God's, I'm thinking God's brains have the clear advantage.

> *If given the choice between racking my brains or God's, I'm thinking God's brains have the clear advantage.*

If things are looking bad for you as a parent, if that deep fear that you're ruining your kids is toppling you over, don't thrash around. The first place you should head is not for the stack of self-help or parenting books, not to the phone, and certainly not to the fridge. All these things (well, not the fridge) are useful, but not as a knee-jerk reaction.

Try to remember that the best knee jerk is a knee bend. Stop right where you are and get down on your knees—physically if you have to. There are times when life is so chaotic that the only way I can find enough of a mental foothold is to literally get down on my knees. I don't think that is the quintessential position of prayer for nothing. There's power in that pose.

Now look up. Fix your eyes on our heavenly Father, on his strength and wisdom, on his mercy and compassion, and get your balance back. Strain to cast your eyes upon the hills. Fight the urge to curl inward.

You'll find—as I did—that you will recover. Forgiveness and understanding will come. Maybe not quickly, maybe not easily, but they will come. And then life's most vital lessons, the stuff of heavenly character, will be yours.

Fear-Facing Questions

Do you fear ruining your children? Do you feel you've already ruined them in some way? Are you in the midst of a colossal battle with a child, estranged somehow, or at your wits' end? How can prayer over the other two-thirds of the picture ease your spirit?

Fear Fighter

When things get sticky, don't flail around. Get down on your knees—physically if you have to. Pray over your part in the mess. Pray over your child's part in it. And trust God for his part in it. Draw a pie chart if it helps to see that you are not even the majority of the situation at hand.

<u>Faith-Finding Verse</u>

Blessed are those who trust in the Lord, whose trust is in the Lord. They shall be like a tree planted by water, sending out its roots by the stream. It shall not fear when heat comes, and its leaves shall stay green; in the year of drought it is not anxious, and it does not cease to bear fruit.

Jeremiah 17:7–8 NRSV

Challenge 3:
Fear Is No Place to Go Alone

Sometimes the Power of Two Is Power Enough

Dark places are scary to navigate alone. There is an old story of a little boy who told his parents he was scared to be alone in his dark room. Their response was the stuff of appropriate, godly parenting. They said, "You are never alone. Jesus is always with you, always protecting you."

"Yeah," replied our scared little hero, "but I need someone with *skin on.*"

Who doesn't want somebody who can hold us, someone with skin on when our rooms get dark and scary?

I went to see *The Lord of the Rings: The Two Towers* (PG–13). I love the sweeping epic of this story, the bravery in the face of daunting odds. And, yes, Viggo Mortenson and Orlando Bloom are mighty easy on the eyes (who *knew* there could be a hunky elf?).

But it is the Frodo character, the tiny hobbit carrying the weight of the world on his shoulders, that stays with me most. Here is someone doing a job for which he is ill-equipped, overwhelmed, and heartbreakingly devoid of quality mentors. It would be hard to dream up someone with more odds against him.

Frodo has no advantages here. Except one: a companion. I discover, when I watch the film closely, that Frodo's companion, Sam, is no more skilled, no more equipped, no more suited to the task than Frodo. He's even rather a dimwit, often making tactical errors that complicate their dire mission. He's well-equipped, however, in matters of morale. Sam teaches us that even when powerless—perhaps *most especially* when powerless—the power of two is power enough.

The moment that resonates with me is the moment when Frodo succumbs yet again to the dark power of the ring he carries. Tolkien's legend imparts the ring with all the hate, malice, and greed of the world. This tiny trinket has a force so dark and so strong that it becomes its own character in the film. It taints all those who come into contact with it, and, while he seems to be less susceptible than others, it also touches Frodo. Actor Elijah Wood excels at his portrayal of this in the film. You see his face transform, watch his eyes take on a dark, shadowy gleam as Frodo gives in to the weight of his task. He lets the ever-present pull take over, tugging him under.

As a parent, how many times have I felt like that in the face of all that is out there to threaten my children on a daily basis? Fear for my children is an ever-present pull, always lurking, ready to join forces with the hundreds of ready conspirators lurking around a parent. In a world of corruption, drugs, war, sex, and violence, just reading the morning headlines can send a dark force creeping over my spirit.

Frodo, in the helpless stupor we parents know far too well, walks up to the edge of his doom. He steps out onto the edge of a tower and lays himself in the crosshairs of the bad guys. He's about to make a mistake of universal proportions. He's falling off the high wire that is his perilous task. No, he's not even falling, he's walking himself right off the wire ... until *whack!* Sam tackles Frodo, knocking him back to safety. Sam stares Frodo in the eye, even when Frodo threatens him, because Sam knows his friend cannot see clearly. He holds Frodo until we watch the tiny hobbit come back from that dark place, and his reason returns.

Haven't you ever needed someone to whack you back from a dark place? I sure have.

Sometimes, though, companionship doesn't require a whack as much as a simple standing alongside. We need our own Sams who have the courage to whack but also the compassion to listen. To be there when we need to cry out, "I can't do this! It's too hard!" Someone whose very presence says, "Yes, it is very, very hard. And I am not sure you can do this either. But one thing I know, you will not try alone."

The other night I called a friend who was having a tough week—a new mother in her first week back at work. I was a working mother for several years, and I remember the agony of those first few weeks. You're pulled in so many different directions you feel you will be dismembered from the strain of it all. Fatigue and hormones wield forces as dark as the ring. Every night I would come home and wail, "I can't do this! It's too hard!" Fear abounded until it began to slip into despair.

Come to think of it, a mother's first week back at work is hardly the only place women groan under that emotion. Labor. Watching your little one wail as you leave them at preschool. Disease. Major behavioral problems. Dying parents. Third-grade math. Single parenting. Elder care. Enduring this week's eleventh preteen, unprovoked crying jag. Colic. Parenting is full of challenges that feel beyond our ability to cope.

My friend's voice was weary and tearful. This was not a situation in which the words, "It'll be all right," would have done one ounce of good. This new mother needed someone not to whack her back from the edge but to stand with her for a few moments, stare into the abyss, accept its size, then gently take her hand and walk her back to safer ground. Over the course of our phone conversation she told me herself—in stories and other shreds of information—that she was a good and capable mother. She was doing right by her child. The weight of her world just kept her from seeing it that night. We talked of the problems she had already solved. There were no solutions I could offer her that she did not already possess. She just needed to be reminded that she had already faced and conquered some of the challenges of motherhood.

My friend's world had proved to be imperfect, and she had not been able to live up to her own expectations. I wanted to say, "Welcome to parenting. A place where perfection is long gone." Ninety percent of her fears will never be realized. Her infant son will still consider her the center of the universe, even if next week is worse than this week. When he is old enough, he will come and hug her for her blunders as readily as my children hug me.

I hope that she has that golden moment someday when the person who whacks her back from the edge is her own child. It is one of the greatest graces of motherhood.

Oh, and by the way, this friend was none other than Melissa, my Yodel-toting savior from Mom's funeral. In the treasured balance of true friendships, we are always given the opportunity to save each other.

Fear-Facing Questions

Is there someone in your life who needs your companionship? Are you in need of a companion yourself? Why might you be afraid of reaching out? How can you reach out to someone this week, even if it can only be by phone?

Fear Fighter

Don't go into the scary places alone. When fear strikes, call on the power of a companion to keep you going. If that means stepping out of your comfort zone to expose a situation, admit a fault, or strike up a new friendship, accept these costs as worth the benefits companionship can give you.

Faith-Finding Verse

Two are better than one, because they have a good return for their work: If one falls down, his friend can help him up!

Ecclesiastes 4:9–10

Parenting Isn't Perfect

The parent-child relationship, by definition, cannot be 100 percent wonderful. Parts of it are hard and awful. Unfortunately, those are often the most important parts of parenting. We need to be reminded, now and then, that parenting takes guts, determination, and persistence. Parenting is hard on the ego, the spirit, the nerves, and the backbone. When I consider some of the most troubled kids I know, I believe many of their troubles stem from a reluctance on the part of their parents to step up to the plate and *be parents*. To make the hard and unpopular choices. To risk making a bad call rather than no call at all. To set limits, to deny their kids things they want, to be mean.

Those of us who work hard for success in parenting yearn to know that our efforts will produce good kids. No such guarantee exists. It is one of life's most heartbreaking paradoxes: Good kids can, and do, go bad. We all know stories of children who have had the best possible parenting and still grew into troubled, ineffective, and even downright dangerous young people.

Here's where the mommy-borne impulse to analyze just makes things worse. When our children's faulty character brings nasty consequences in their lives, we're quick to blame ourselves. Did we foster that irresponsibility by not giving them enough chores at home? Did the one time I went away on short notice create that abandonment issue? We instantly jump to "Where did we go wrong?" because that propagates the comfortable myth that *we might still be able to fix it*. Because good parents should be able to fix it, right?

The heartbreaking (and perhaps freeing) answer to that question must be, "Not always." Our children are not little clones of us. We've made enormous strides this decade in coming to understand the chemical individuality of each human being and how many challenging behaviors have physical roots beyond our control as parents. Our children are individuals who make choices of how to respond to the love and training we give them, and sometimes those choices are bad ones. They are the furthest thing from what we would choose for our children. I'd bet each one of us knows a great family with an unthinkably rebellious child—and it breeds fear because it reminds us how little control we ultimately have as parents.

> *We instantly jump to "Where did we go wrong?" because that propagates the comfortable myth that we might still be able to fix it.*

To see a well-loved, well-trained child go wrong is heartbreaking. We watch their parents grieve and weep over the lost lives of their children, and we weep with them. We grieve that so much of it is out of our hands. We grieve that our parenting is only part of the equation.

Every parent of faith sweats it out over their children's salvation. Many mothers wrote me to tell me one of their biggest fears is that their child, despite every effort to the contrary, will walk away from faith in Jesus Christ. Most of us with multiple children have the children who latched on to faith right away but still have that one child who keeps us hanging on by our spiritual fingernails. The one who just doesn't seem to be drawn to it. The one who decides to go very wrong before heading back in the right direction. Or the one who never heads back at all.

It is difficult—and yet important—to realize that winning our children to Christ is not our responsibility. I was not led to Christ by my parents. It is God's high holy prerogative to decide when, if, and by whom our children come to faith. That's not saying that we should not do *everything in our power* to point them in the right direction, to pray and work and teach and train them to love and serve God. But we do not push our children to God—God draws them to himself. God's will is God's will.

Heartbreaking as it may be to endure, we can find some hope in remembering the very strong possibility that a child's king-size sinfulness may craft him or her to be a God-sized proponent of the faith. God loves unlikely candidates. Saul of Tarsus was Christian Enemy #1 before God decided it was time for him to get with the program. Saul's nasty past prepared him to become "Paul" and to be the powerful tool of God that he became.

God's plan for our children is not ours to craft. It is ours to pray over, care for, and maybe even lament over, but not to own.

Chapter 8

THE AUDIENCE

"I worry about what other moms think of my housekeeping."

"I'm afraid no one really likes me. They're all just faking it."

"I am scared of spending time alone in the basement."

*"I'm afraid we'll encounter a medical problem
that I won't be able to handle."*

Who's Watching? Why Does it Matter?

Parenting would be so much easier if children weren't involved.

It would be marvelous if we could take a moment to catch our breath, take time to plan, prepare, and make excellent decisions without them underfoot every waking moment. If they weren't watching us all the time, it would be a much less challenging job.

Parents, though, are on stage under scrutiny 24/7/365. We know the power of our visibility, our example—and we know that it can be for good and for bad. That makes us wary. When I began to poll mothers about their greatest fears, the number one answer—by a landslide I hadn't expected—was fear over the backlash from our own mistakes.

Why? Because we know they're watching us. Our children are looking to us for inspiration, modeling, and guidance. They are our audience as we walk this parenting high wire. We need to remember that in times of fear as much as everything else. Because you and I both know *if Mama ain't calm, ain't nobody calm.* We set the tone; we set the response; we fuel the chaos or supply the calm.

For the most part, I take on the mantra of "actions speak louder than words" with open eyes. In calm situations, most mothers can act wisely on this pedestal of parenting. That's why I *sneak into* the pantry to eat chocolate chips right out of the bag. (You shouldn't model that kind of bad behavior out in the open, right?) We know that how we live teaches our children how to live. Simply put, getting my own act together—or at least modeling the attempt if not the achievement of "togetherness"—shows my kids how to get their own acts together.

Now turn the heat up, raise the stakes, and strike up a crisis. Nine times out of ten all that good sense flees the scene.

We'd all prefer that anxiety not hit us in front of our children, but we don't have much choice. Mothers are rarely alone. When life's crises hit, they'll rarely catch us in the luxury of privacy. So how we deal with fear when our kids are watching poses a major parenting issue.

Most mothers can act wisely on this pedestal of parenting. That's why I sneak into the pantry to eat chocolate chips right out of the bag.

Hey, what's a good aerialist without an audience? Well, she's rehearsing, that's what she is—and our life is no rehearsal.

Challenge 1:
Mom Is the Biggest Fear Factor of All
How to Make the Most of Your Next Car Crash

There was an episode in my life when, by the grace of God, I acted wisely in my fear. I've taken some time to examine this memorable moment, looking for the good stuff so I can learn from my experience.

My husband, Jeff, likes cars. I mean he *really* likes cars. He owns a nifty little sports car (okay, it has a back seat—I insisted). Once a year the kids and I go away with Jeff to a precision driving school event and play Dad's cheering section. Jeff supports me through all the nutty stuff I choose to do, so I'm glad of the chance to be supportive of him.

I wasn't so glad one year.

There are no grandstands on autocross tracks, so you pick a spot somewhere on the infield and basically picnic. At driving school events like this one, each driver gets quite a few chances at time on the track—this isn't something you can learn in the Denny's parking lot. When you're watching without benefit of bleachers, however, you can only see one section of the track. This means we essentially stand around for a while, jump up and down when Jeff's car goes by, then stand around until we see his car again, etc. The trip around the track takes approximately two minutes.

Once, Jeff took a bit longer that two minutes. Quite a lot longer. And the fact that I wasn't seeing his white car come around the bend with all the others was starting to unravel my nerves. I didn't do a great job of staying calm. They have a system of colored flags at the school, and a yellow flag means something has happened on the track, and all

202

the other students need to slow down. When the yellow flag went up, I was not a bastion of calm motherhood. In actuality, Jeff had just spun a bit on a turn (to be expected I understand) and needed a few minutes to get his car in the right position again before he came back to our little camp in the infield. No big deal. A little mud in the tires, nothing more. When he explained, Mandy shot me one of those, "See, Mom. Why'd you get all weird on us?" looks. I realized I'd just shown the kids a fine example of worry over nothing.

Well, okay, almost nothing. I *am* human, and he *was* in a car on a racetrack.

Last year the scenario repeated itself. As the lap completed and Jeff's car was not back on time, I caught Mandy's eye. "You're not going to get all crazy again are you, Mom?" was her suspicious inquiry.

"No, dear," I replied, forcibly injecting calm disinterest into my voice. "Dad knows what he's doing."

Jeff *does* know what he's doing. He's an excellent driver. What's more, because of his interest in the sport and time behind the wheel, if something should happen, Jeff is far more capable of negotiating a car out of control than most drivers on the road. It's more of a controlled situation than the L.A. freeway. Those drivers have more safety gear on than most off-roaders, and they're not even hitting highway speeds.

None of that meant a thing when I heard the following over the PA system: "Would the wife of Jeff Pleiter please come to the first aid station." Ah, there's nothing like a gallon of adrenaline gushing through your veins to ensure a memorable day at driving school.

I kid you not, the first place my eyes darted was to Mandy, who was looking *straight at me.* I knew in that split second that she would base her entire reaction on my reaction. How it was all going to flow from here was entirely up to me and whether or not I could keep my cool.

I took as deep a breath as I could manage. Then I saw the ambulance.

Cool was flying out the window when a couple of men pulled up in a truck labeled (no kidding) "The Rescue Guys" and one said in that *we-know-this-is-going-to-freak-you-out-but-let's-all-try-to-stay-calm* voice, "You need to follow us."

> I took as deep a breath as I could manage. Then I saw the ambulance.

This made trying to stay calm even harder. The very first thing that went through my mind, though, right alongside all those scenarios worthy of *ER*, was *the kids are watching me.* Mandy's stare sunk straight into my nervous system. It's fascinating how instantly and competently my instincts took over. I knew—without even consciously thinking it through—that the kids had to come with me, but that they shouldn't go inside the ambulance.

I took each one by the hand and we began to walk behind the rescue guys. That, I admit, was the hardest part. With every step I told myself, *Do not faint. Do not throw up.* And, in the rather sick mental camera that every writer has, I thought, *Remember what this feels like for your book. Take notes. Watch yourself.*

I was also talking to the kids at that point, but for the life of me I can't tell you what I said. I only know I tried to keep my voice level and sensible. And I attempted to keep breathing.

I made a surprising number of calculations and decisions in a matter of minutes. I knew not to leave the children with the two dozen compassionate people who offered as we slowly made our way through a tunnel of gaping faces toward the ambulance. I knew they needed to sit nearby, with someone they recognized, while I climbed into that ambulance to see what had become of my husband. My brain analyzed that if something were very, very wrong, they should not be with strangers if my attention needed to be 100 percent on Jeff.

Make no mistake, I didn't pretend not to be afraid. I had every reason on earth to be afraid. My children knew something was wrong. The faces of every person around us echoed that fact. What I hope I showed them that day, however, was the difference between fear and panic.

We held hands and walked together, and I think I repeated our family crisis motto: "It looks like we're going to have ourselves an adventure." We took it one step at a time. I told them that only I could go inside the ambulance to talk with Daddy, but that I'd come right back out as soon as I could and tell them what had happened. Then I climbed into the ambulance and prepared to wince at pools of blood and other horrors.

> What I hope I showed them that day was the difference between fear and panic.

What I found was a very intact but soundly immobilized man saying, "It's all right, Allie. I'm fine. Really, I'm okay."

"No, you're not okay," I replied. "You're strapped to a backboard inside an ambulance. That does not qualify as 'okay.'" At least I think I said that. I certainly was thinking it at the time. I'm sure, "Honey, I love you and it will all work out fine," would have been the proper good wifely thing to say, but it is deeply ingrained in my personality to fight my fear by wisecracking in a tense situation. (Note: This is not necessarily a *good* thing.)

After several minutes of evaluation and planning, it was decided that Jeff would go the nearest hospital to get checked out because he had suffered a bad bump to the head. Seeing the big scrape in his helmet didn't do wonders for my nerves, I admit. I gave Jeff a quick kiss on the cheek and climbed back out to undertake the complicated process of packing up and getting ourselves out of the track behind the ambulance. The woman who said, "You might want to make sure you don't go by the car on the way out," was absolutely correct, even if it did send my fertile imagination roaring into action. I took her advice and avoided the car, which had been declared a disturbing "undrivable." *Wait, we're okay, things are good, no blood*, kept running through my mind, although a litany of potential back, neck, and head injuries was running right behind it.

I was as honest as possible with the kids. In truth, I didn't have the spare emotional energy to mask anything. I told them Dad needed to see a doctor, that the ambulance would take him, and that we'd go to the hospital right behind them. I gave them each jobs to do and explained, "Mom isn't thinking very clearly right now; you're going to have to help me." They did. They remembered directions, they prayed with me as we drove down the highway, they packed things up and even thought of ways to amuse themselves once we got to the emergency room. In short, we handled it quite well. Jeff was fine, and the hospital trip proved only precautionary. Everything—and everyone—turned out okay.

I'd like to think my children learned from our car crash experience. I hoped they saw their mother trying to take a touchy situation one step at a time, trying not to jump to conclusions, but yet giving the danger of the situation the respect it deserved. We learned how to support each other. I learned that they, young as they were, could still be a comfort and a help to me in a tricky situation. I hope they learned Mom can be very afraid but still keep a level head (occasionally). I learned the double-edged sword of an offspring audience: We bear the burden of setting the example, but they can offer surprising comfort and companionship.

Sure, it *might* have been less traumatic to keep them as far as possible from the potential ugliness of Dad's injuries.

But I don't think that's why God designed the family. Our family was in a tight spot, and they are part of our family. In healthy ways, they needed to be part of this. I could no more shut them out of it than I could let them into all of it as if they were adults. Dr. Cartmell wisely advises parents that it's important to allow our children access to such information—*but only after we've filtered it.*

For example, it was wise to let them see the ambulance and to let them know that Dad was inside. But it would have been unwise to let them climb in there with me. If Jeff had been seriously injured—bloodied, banged up, in danger of lasting physical harm—the wise thing to do would have been to stay with Jeff until we both had enough of a grip on things to be able to filter the information. Not necessarily until I was calm, for that would have been an unachievable goal, but until I could see clearly enough to know what information was appropriate for my children to hear.

They needed to see the crisis through my filter—even though my filter was a mighty scared one. The filter is what makes the difference between telling them, "Dad needs to see a doctor," and telling them, "Dad may have undetected brain damage." Sure, both thoughts were racing through my head, but the wisdom of the moment was knowing which *not* to share. That filter is what allows the children to be present but not entrenched.

Installing that filter is our job as parents. If we are in such an emotional state that filtering isn't possible, then keeping our children out of a situation is prudent. Not letting them inside the ambulance, so to speak. The practical application of this is that you should not blindly share information or experiences with your children if you can help it (and yes, sometimes it simply *cannot* be helped).

Conversely, it is wrong to hide a crisis or threat from your children completely. They are almost always sensitive enough to know something is wrong. To deny that and pretend everything is hunky-dory only gives their fertile imaginations an open door to conjure up something that may be even worse than the actual situation at hand. Denial is not protection.

Instead, call upon prayer, friends, and even the grace of a bit of time to restore part of your composure. Another adult, or your heavenly Father, can handle the raw facts and help you sort things out a bit. Your children very likely cannot and should not.

> *It is wrong to hide a crisis or threat from your children completely. They are almost always sensitive enough to know something is wrong.*

When you accept the responsibility to bring your children into the situation in a way that is appropriate to their age and sensitivity, you allow the family to be a family. To do the things that families do: offer support and encouragement and participate in the full mess of life.

To shoo the children away would have denied them the valuable lesson we all learned that day: How to support each other when the chips are down. And the only place to learn that lesson is smack in the middle of falling chips.

Fear-Facing Questions

Can you recall a time when you used your parental filter wisely in a fearful situation? Is there a time when you didn't? How would you change how you reacted? Can you learn from one experience to improve another?

Fear Fighter

Install your fear filter. Before you share the raw information about a fearful situation, make sure you can relate it in a responsible way. If not, call upon another adult to help you, distance your children from the situation for a brief time, and pray for wisdom, discernment, and guidance.

Then bring your children into the situation in ways that can let them show you they care.

Faith-Finding Verse

When I am afraid, I will trust in you. In God, whose word I praise, in God I trust; I will not be afraid.
Psalm 56:3–4

Challenge 2:
Good Fears Can Go Bad

Why Not to Join the Mothers' High Anxiety Society

No one would argue against the fact that part of the parental role is to teach our children caution. But certainly none of us want to teach them fear.

Until I began talking with several mental health professionals for this book, though, I was unaware how much fear is *learned*—directly or indirectly. The medical profession is coming to understand that a certain propensity toward anxiety can indeed be genetically inherited. Nervous parents do, in fact, tend to have nervous children. But most mental health professionals will tell you that's only a small part of the picture. Often nervous parents *train* children to be nervous.

Our fears give our children fears. What's more, our responses to fears can sometimes yield results that are the exact opposites of our good intentions. It stopped me dead in my tracks to realize courage isn't just virtuous; it also makes good parenting sense.

One doctor on our expert panel shared an example with me. She had counseled a woman who, for perfectly understandable reasons, chose to opt her middle-school daughter out of many coed social functions. *There will be time enough to learn about boys,* this mother thought. And what mother of a twelve-year-old girl doesn't cringe a bit when the talk turns to boys, "going out," who likes whom, etc.

Sure we remember the social complications of middle school, but the world seems like such a different place than when we were in seventh grade. Kids seem to be doing all the bad stuff so much younger. For the first time ever, my children's *elementary* school had to issue a dress code this year. It prohibited high heels, spaghetti straps, and other things I associate only with older girls. Experts advise us to talk about drugs, sex, and alcohol with our children at age *nine!* Sex at nine? Drugs before ten? *Gulp*, it feels like a jungle out there! Who could blame this mother for wanting to hold the tide back just a little longer? Don't we all?

I was astounded to discover that despite the advantages of keeping her daughter from lots of social interaction with boys (the girl would, after all, still see them every day at school), there were real dangers to this mother's attitude. Why? Because the mom's boundaries were drawn *out of fear*. Fear that a boy would do something inappropriate.

Now wait a minute; that seems like a reasonable fear if you ask me. Well, yes and no. As the doctor began to explain the outcomes of such restrictions, the light bulb in my head went on. What message—subtle, mind you, but there all the same—does that restriction send? We stay away from things that are bad or dangerous. Hence, the message here—intended or not—is that *boys are dangerous.*

Now anyone who has spent any time at all with a group of seventh-grade boys knows they are unruly, excitable, and drawn to shocking behavior, so that doesn't seem too far a jump. Except when we allow the caution to rule our own behavior. "Boys are dangerous, so don't go near them if you can help it" was the message this mom passed down to her daughter. Now that's not entirely wrong—girls should know that the best way to stay *out* of trouble is not to get yourself *in* a situation where trouble is likely. But here was a mom who kept her daughter out of supervised, even church-sponsored, social situations. The message she sent her daughter was that *boys are so dangerous that you can't protect yourself.*

Project this idea down a few years to the inevitable boy-girl interaction. There's been no learning curve, no adjustment, no opportunity to gain the discernment that helps us separate true fears from false ones. This girl has subtly but continually learned that boys have power over her and she has to alter her actions because of that power. The mom's fear—which went beyond caution—taught her daughter that she must change her actions (i.e., not go to some events) because she can't protect herself. In essence, she learned that *boys have more power than she does.*

So what happens when a boy pushes her physically or does something inappropriate? This girl is less likely to stand up for herself, less likely to fight back, *more likely to get into the very trouble her mother sought to avoid.* Why? Because *most* boys *aren't* dangerous, but this girl hasn't learned to (1) sort out the good from the bad and (2) defend herself.

No mother on earth would intentionally set out to do this. So how did it happen? This mother had taken a perfectly reasonable caution (which demands we teach cautionary measures) and allowed it to grow out of proportion. She's done a tremendous amount of *protecting* but very little *preparing.* This mother allowed her fear to run unchecked—to go from fearing *bad* boys to fearing *all* boys. While rape or abuse or something else horrible may never happen to her daughter, the sad truth is that by giving in to fear, the mother has *increased* the chances of it happening. This really made me stop and think. It's vital to realize that *fear let loose leads us to unhealthy choices.*

The healthiest thing we can do is to deal with our fears rather than run from them, because in the running we often make things worse. Keeping your daughter from going out on a date when she's ten is sensible. But she's going to go out on a date some day. Yes, it's scary to think of her in some teenage boy's car while he slyly sneaks his arm around her waist. There's not a mother on the planet who doesn't fear for her daughter's sexual purity. But if in our determination to shield her from the bad parts of the world for as long as possible we teach her that *all boys are bad and she can't be in the same room with them because heaven knows what they'll do,* we will rob her of the ability to learn why some boys ought to be avoided but others can make fine, healthy friends. About how, when, and why "being with a boy" becomes "a date." There must be a balance between protection and preparation.

You can bet I'm nervous about my daughter dating. All mothers of girls worry about such things. This story did wake me up, however, to the consequences of letting that fear run away with my good sense. It's the strongest endorsement for maternal courage I know. Courage is what enables us to balance our urge to protect with a call to prepare. We need to face our fears as mothers not just because it's good mental health but because our children are watching.

> Courage is what enables us to balance our urge to protect with a call to prepare. We need to face our fears as mothers not just because it's good mental health but because our children are watching.

When our children see us give in to an unreasonable fear or see us run from things that frighten us, we teach our children that those things have power. And do you know what? In some cases that's a good thing. Cars in the street really do have power. It's right that our children learn to fear them. We seek to teach our children to fear the Lord because God really has power. Guns and diseases and sin and criminals have power. But are we teaching our children to be powerless in the face of these things?

We can sort this out by remembering that fear has advantages and disadvantages. There are bad fears and there are good fears. Dr. David Burns suggests an effective exercise to help us sort out such fears. As you stare down any given fear, take a sheet of paper and draw a line down the middle. On the left write "Disadvantages," on the right, "Advantages."[15] To Burns's instructions, I'd add saying a prayer for wisdom and guidance at this point. Now take a while and truly examine the value of what you fear.

Let's take, for example, the surprisingly common fear that your children will grow up to hate you, that you'll make a parenting error from which they'll never recover and for which they'll never forgive you. There might be several advantages to that fear. Try to write down your thoughts just as they come to you, sensible or not. For example, knowing you can do harm might encourage you to be as wise as possible in your choices. It feels like better parenting to care whether your kids like you. This fear might keep you from overreacting in anger. It may drive you to take a parenting class or to seek out the advice and fellowship of parents you admire. That fear indicates you value your children's mental health and your relationship with them. It means you want to be a good parent, to have your kids think of you as a force for good in their lives.

Now take a look at the disadvantages. Wanting your children to like everything you do could lead you to get soft on an issue when you need to be tough. It can lead you to continually seek the approval of your children. It can frighten you into inactivity if you become so afraid of scarring your kids that you end up more befriending your children than parenting them. It adds stress and tension to your life, making you second-guess every choice you make. This should give you a clearer picture of your fear and how it can work for good or bad in your life and the lives of your children.

I must emphasize that you *must* do this exercise in writing. It doesn't work if you just try to go through the advantages and disadvantages in your head. (Believe me, I tried.

It simply doesn't work.) This is because you won't recognize an illogical thought until you see it in writing. For example, your brain will easily accept the thought, *My kids will hate me when they're adults.* It's crossed the minds of every mother on earth. Yet when you see it on paper, you begin to recognize the drastic nature of such a thought. You can look for evidence to disprove or prove the thought. Putting this kind of analysis on paper somehow gives us the distance to really examine our thoughts and feelings and see them for the fact or fiction they are.

I believe God will honor your examination of the situation and offer you wisdom. Ask him to show you the balance of those advantages and disadvantages, to part your emotional Red Sea and show you the secure path. He has promised to give us wisdom and counsel if we but ask. He is a parent himself and has had his children go about as wrong as children can go. God knows things about you, your children, and the situation that you may never see or may simply not know yet.

What's worth fearing and what's not? Our kids learn by watching us.

Fear-Facing Questions

What fear about your child's development makes you most frightened? Does it have the capacity to distort your thinking like the mother of the middle-school girl? What can you do to gain a clearer view?

Fear Fighter

Draw a line down the center of a sheet of paper and label the columns: "This Fear's Advantages" and "This Fear's Disadvantages." Write down your thoughts on the positive and negative outcomes of your fear and the way you are reacting to it. Doing this on paper helps you recognize the true thoughts from the emotional reactions. Then you can decide if the fear is really worth having and take steps to live with it or overcome that fear.

Faith-Finding Verse

God keeps his promise, and will not allow you to be tested beyond your power to remain firm; at the time you are put to the test, he will give you the strength to endure it, and so provide you with a way out.

1 Corinthians 10:13 TEV

Challenge 3:
Some Fears Can Keep Us from Good Things
Give the Gift of Getting Over It

It is good to teach our children caution. It is wise to train them to respect danger and not to be reckless with their lives, the lives of others, or the resources God gave them. You've heard it a dozen times in this book: Some fears are *worth* having. Some fears will never leave us—and *should* never leave us.

Then, though, there are fears that are worth conquering. These fears—foolish fears, if you will—aren't valuable. These fears may keep us and our children from experiencing good things. We don't want to teach our children such fears. Instead, the best gift we can give our children is teaching them *how to get over it*.

Let's look at a classic example: stage fright. I play the harp. I really enjoy it. There aren't a whole lot of harpists in every neighborhood, so it's kind of a unique, neat thing. I also have a wicked case of musician's stage fright. It makes very little sense. I can speak in front of thousands of people, feel my pulse rise, and recognize it for the valuable surge of energy that it is, and go onstage without a shred of fear.

Stick me behind a harp and in front of even three people and I go to pieces. And what's that done? It's kept me from playing in public. Which is dumb, because what's the use of playing an instrument if no one can hear you play? Yes, I know all about the joy of playing purely for me or for God, but you and I both know that's only half the purpose of music. And, as a friend recently told me, how many chances in life does the average person get to hear live harp music?

The situation is really no different than our frightened mother from the last chapter. I have given an unreasonable fear power over my actions. I like performing. I like an audience (maybe too much). Giving in to this fear is a self-fulfilling prophecy, because any musician will tell you there are some things you can *only* learn in performance. I am, in effect, hampering myself as a musician because I'm worried about myself as a musician. I'm letting my fear trick me into actions (like avoiding performance situations) that feel like they're protecting me but actually are perpetuating the problem—if not making it worse.

For quite some time I let this get the best of me and turned down request after request to play in church. For the brief time that Mandy played the harp, I discovered the child has not one ounce of stage fright, musically. She is my opposite—unworried about playing an instrument on stage even though her skills are far below mine but not too eager to get up and speak.

It is a good and powerful thing for our children to see we have fears. It shows them that having fear is a part of life. Courageous people aren't people who don't fear; they are people who don't let fear *stop* them. We do our children a tremendous disservice if they don't watch us *deal* with our fears.

> It is a good and powerful thing for our children to see we have fears. It shows them that having fear is a part of life. Courageous people aren't people who don't fear; they are people who don't let fear stop them.

I have come to realize that I am teaching Amanda avoidance. I am teaching her that stage fright has power. The power to keep me from doing something that actually would benefit me. This is a particularly potent example because while our stage frights are polar opposites (speaking versus performing), it shows us that *it is the fear itself* that does the teaching. Mandy will not learn to speak in public by watching me, because she can easily see that I'm not afraid. Yet, it cannot be ignored that I am bolstering *her* type of stage fright by allowing *mine* to win.

The only way out for both of us was for me to "get over it" in plain sight. Because, you see, if I don't, I am teaching her "you can't get over it." And what if I deprive her of some great talent or gift some day because she gives in to her own fear? Not only that, but I truly, truly believe that conquering fear is its own reward.

Armed with determination, I made new goals this year when my old harp teacher moved away and I needed to find a new one. When shopping for the new teacher, my number one objective was to get over this performance anxiety. For three months we worked on it. I'm pleased to say that recently I played in church for the first time in over a year, even though it took a boatload of preparation and I was shaking in my shoes.

Mandy saw all of that preparation, all of that fear-fighting. She watched me play with her in the room, watched me tape myself and listen to it until I could do so without wincing, and even came with me to set the harp up the night before. And she was my biggest cheerleader. What a gift that was.

Sometimes you discover that your kids are not only your audience but also your most valuable resource. This truth was another of the lessons I learned at my mother's passing. You've already heard about all the likely stress of the funeral arrangements and such. The unlikely fright of that week, however, was an everyday task of a car trip.

I had elected to spend the ten days after Mom's funeral beginning the arduous task of liquidating her estate. (It was the summertime and the last stretch of uncommitted time I would have for a while.) Mom lived near the beach in Connecticut, so I planned to spend mornings working on the estate and spend the afternoons giving the kids a taste of salt water. There was a mountain of things to do: sorting through photos, clothes, and jewelry, getting mail forwarded, canceling subscriptions, a million tiny details.

That time also gave me the opportunity to drive a few hours with the kids to see my dear friend Becky, who lived in the neighboring state of New Jersey. Becky had been a very close friend back in Chicago but recently had moved to the East Coast. It had been the roughest of weeks, and all I wanted to do was sit in her kitchen and drink coffee until I could manage a laugh again. I would have crawled across broken glass to get to her, I was so thirsty for her companionship.

So why was I, who had driven alone across the country with my children on a ten-day car trip (to Becky's house, as a matter of fact!) just three months earlier, suddenly terrified of managing two hours on the New Jersey Turnpike? Who knows? I'm not even sure there has to be a reason. When you've spent the last five days coping at the end of your wits, you don't need a monumental challenge to send you over the edge. A tiny one will do just fine.

So over the edge I went. Even with a map in front of me and a set of crystal-clear directions, the drive loomed like Mt. Everest, miles above my capabilities. I sat on my mother's bed, maps spread across the bedspread we'd bought together last Christmas, and wailed. I have never in my entire life been more afraid to get behind the wheel of a car. Jeff had returned to Chicago, going back to work after taking nearly a week off to be with me in Connecticut, and I called him in tears. He offered what help he could, but what help was there?

My children couldn't drive me to New Jersey. But they could watch me let an ordinary task—a foolish fear—stop me from something I very much wanted to do. It was a real dilemma at a time when I didn't have a whole host of extra coping skills.

Mandy and CJ came in and crawled onto the bed with me. I was too emotional, too strung out, to hide my fear from them. It could have been a bad situation where I failed to use my parental filter. I could have allowed them too closely into the deeper, very adult problem of large-scale grief. It could have been a bad experience. But it wasn't.

It wasn't a bad experience because children, in all their innocence, have the capacity to recognize a foolish fear—often before we adults do. My children knew that Becky's house was a good thing and that driving there wasn't scary. So they became my best sources of courage.

My own children told me I could do this task. They talked about the car trip we'd taken just that year and how we'd overcome far larger challenges than getting our little trio to New Jersey. "But Mom, you drove from *Chicago* to Becky's house. Connecticut is much closer."

My kids watched their mother go to pieces; then they put her back together again. Why? Even though I thought I hadn't filtered the situation for them, I actually had. By the grace of God, I managed to focus on the *piece* of the problem that needed solving. Sure, my mother had just died. Life was quite messy. Lots of bigger problems were looming above my head. "Trouble comes," Dr. Cartmell advises, "when parents don't employ that filter and treat their children like confidants." It would have been unfair and unwise to unload the full scope of my problems on them. They could not be expected to cope with estate planning, mortality, or the particular grief of becoming parentless. In reality, none of those problems have easy, quick solutions.

But I just needed to get to New Jersey—at least just for today. That, my kids could deal with.

That piece is an important distinction—and a key reason why my kids didn't go to pieces right alongside me. While death and estate planning and becoming parentless were certainly contributing to the problem, they weren't the actual problem at hand. Somehow God gave me the grace to see and invite my children into just the piece that needed solving at that moment—making the drive.

Second, I let them help. I wonder, in hindsight, if I would have let them help me if I had been in better emotional health. I would have second-guessed my filter, extrapolated a dozen reasons why they needed to see Mom in control. Had it been in another situation, I probably wouldn't have shared my trip-phobia. I probably would have fallen back on the time-honored standby of, "It's fine, Mom will take care of this."

Under those circumstances, we might still have made it to New Jersey, but with a lot more stress. Instead, I allowed them to come onto my side of the problem. I let them see me struggling with it—at a level appropriate to them—and allowed them to help. To use our performance metaphor, I let them give the audience energy back to me so we could all have a better performance.

We made it to New Jersey, and everyone was so much the better for fellowship with dear friends. I sat at Becky's kitchen table and drank coffee until my life felt the smallest bit normal. And I thanked God, over and over, for the encouragement.

How did my precious children help me make it to New Jersey? It was their idea to stop at no less than *three* Dunkin' Donuts stores along the way until the scary drive transformed itself into a two-hour episode of "who can find the next donut store?"

No, my children could not really help me grieve the loss of my last remaining parent. But they *could* help me drive to New Jersey.

Death and grief, serious injury from a car crash; these are real, powerful fears. They are things that are worth fearing. Driving two hours to New Jersey or playing harp in public is not. I'll be the first to tell you, though, that both *feel* real.

The lesson here wasn't about a harp or a car crash or a speech. It was about life, about why risk is a good thing and why some obstacles ought to be torn down. It is my prayer that by watching these episodes, and the many, many more to come, my children learn to face and fight certain fears.

I don't want to teach the power of fear; I want to teach the power of courage. I want them to learn that while I cannot control events, while I cannot guarantee the safety of those I love, I can control my response. I can allow an event or challenge to make me stronger, to be a tool available to God to further teach me and to strengthen us as a family.

Fear-Facing Questions

You knew this was coming: What fear do your children need to see you conquer? Sure it's hard, but can you use the potential for their growth as motivation for your own courage? What about your own personal growth? How would everyone gain?

Fear Fighter

Courage is its own reward. When deciding to face a fear, make a list of all that your children will gain from watching you face it. Visualize wonderful experiences they will have because they've been freed by your example. Let such benefits motivate you and build your courage. Allow your children the joy of cheering Mom on to victory.

Faith-Finding Verse

He who began a good work in you will carry it on to completion until the day of Christ Jesus.

Philippians 1:6

The Show Must Go On

If we are on display as parents all the time, then we'd better be on our best behavior all the time, right? This kind of pressure is what makes parenting so exhausting. I quipped earlier that "parenting would be so much easier if children weren't involved," and we all laugh at that line because it's *so true*. Each one of us has felt we could be much better parents if we didn't have to be parents *so much*. Parenthood's constancy is sometimes the stuff of Chinese water torture. One drop won't hurt, but 827 in a row will drive you over the edge.

The truth that conquers stage fright is also the truth that takes the pressure off parenting. My harp teacher told me, "No one who listens to you is looking for errors." My head can understand that concept, but my heart (and, more precisely, my heart rate) has yet to embrace it. I do not critically analyze music when I hear it—I simply let it sink into my spirit and enjoy it. Someone could blow a piece and need to start completely over, and I'd still get something from the music. Why can't I let that knowledge get rid of my fear of making an error in front of an audience?

I believe parents suffer from a form of parental stage fright. All the parent-bashing pop psychology out there has led us to believe that we can't make mistakes in front of our children. We've accepted that we must be flawless parents 90 percent of the time or the results will be disastrous.

I hope the last section and this one have helped you to believe that's not true. Our children are no more eager to condemn us than any audience goes to a concert in order to criticize the musician. No, they're waiting, listening, eager to extend grace and pull good things from our performance despite any errors. Yes, they are watching, and yes, they are learning, but they are not critics (teen years possibly excepted). How easily we think our children are watching to nail us for our errors, when they are really watching to love us for our efforts.

One night toward the end of my high-wire lessons, my teachers were part of a circus performance. I took the whole family. We had a marvelous time watching all the amazing things my teachers and their talented colleagues performed. I couldn't believe the human body could do some of the things I saw.

Toward the end of the show, my teacher Tony was attempting a truly astounding feat. He failed on the first attempt, slipping off the pole that was to be his landing spot and tumbling nearly into the lap of an audience member. There were the expected gasps from the crowd. For a moment, despite the costumes and make-up, we were all reminded that he was *human*, not magical.

> How easily we think our children are watching to nail us for our errors, when they are really watching to love us for our efforts.

That realization made it all the more wonderful when Tony landed it on the next attempt. I realized that we cheered *all the more* for his efforts *because* we had watched the first error. It reminded us of the spectacular nature of what Tony does, made more spectacular by the knowledge that he is merely one of us. We didn't just watch him that night, we cheered him on. Changed from spectators to encouragers and celebrants. We became the very best of what an audience can be, which is why live theater is a magical experience like no other.

Oh, if we could only be the Tonys of parenting. Moms who are careful, striving, but not so nervous that we cannot fall off the wire in front of our children and get back up again only to succeed all the more. If I could let that truth sink the long distance from my head to my heart, I'd play my harp joyfully anytime anyone asked. If I could let that truth sink into my heart, I'd parent with so much more love and so much less fear.

Chapter 9

THE VIEW

"I'm afraid I will miss a monumental moment. Blow a chance
in their development that I won't ever get back again."

"I fear that because we've rationalized financially
for me to stay home, we'll end up broke and my
children won't have what they need."

"I worry we made a bad call in allowing them to have
so much TV, computers, and video games. What if
they're forever addicted to video entertainment?"

"Everyone says 'choose your battles wisely.'
What if I don't? What if by the time I'm aware
that I've chosen the wrong battle, it's too late?"

Look Down. No, Don't Look Down. No, Look Down. No . . .

What's the first thing everyone says about a high spot? "Oh, will you look at the view from up here!" The view is what makes altitude a double-edged sword. We can see farther, but that also means we can *fall* farther. It gives perspective, but it increases danger.

It's rather like standing on the viewing platform of the Empire State Building. If we look out, we can see for miles in all directions and can get a marvelous sense of New York City's spectacular sprawl. We behold the beauty of the skyline we can't hope to appreciate when standing on the ground. It is an amazing sight.

Lean over and look down, however, and things start to change. Suddenly you feel the building do that unsettling bit of swaying that all skyscrapers do in the wind. Your brain calculates just how far off the ground you are. You notice all the spiky fencing around the platform, which reminds you this would be a surefire place to end your life if you were so inclined. Your remember all those urban legends about people throwing pennies off the Empire State Building that build up so much speed on the descent that they kill those they hit below.

Forget the panoramic view now. You're done sightseeing, thank you very much, and you creep back into the safety of the lobby and welcome the popping of your ears as the elevator coasts down the eighty-six floors. Nothing has changed, except where you cast your eyes. Views can wield a powerful influence.

Most mothers get caught up in a view of parenting that feels much like the scary height of the Empire State Building. It's hard for us to enjoy the view of our parenting journey and the particular beauty of helping to craft a human life because we're so easily hypnotized by the dangers. Because there *are* so many dangers.

Parenting isn't safe! Eek—don't look down! Yet, we *have* to look down. Then, when we look at the dangers inherent in raising healthy kids today and muster the courage to parent, it's *real* courage. The kind of courage that will hold up when things get sticky because it recognizes that things *are* going to get sticky. The kind of courage that isn't built on false securities or comfortable denial but on true strength.

> If you're worried about the quality of your parenting, that means you are parenting. You are not defective; you're effective.

If looking down makes you nervous, congratulations. You're not a coward; you're smart enough to see the truth. See if you can get yourself to welcome that tension, to embrace that concern as the sign of a caring parent rather than the mark of a defective mother. I've said it earlier, but it bears repeating: If you're worried about the quality of your parenting, that means you *are* parenting. You are not *defective;* you're *effective.*

From where I sit and from the experts I've consulted, the only truly bad parent is the one who won't get involved. Let me repeat that: The only truly bad parent is the one who won't get involved.

Sure, it's much harder to take your parenting seriously. It requires much more effort, more emotional pain, more sacrifice, more everything. Your fear is actually something positive, for it shows you are respecting the importance of the job you undertake. What makes the difference is *where you cast your eyes.*

Looking down means we recognize vital life lessons are coming for us and our children. While we must not live under the tyranny of the "teachable moment," we should pay attention to what's going on in life.

Looking up means we recognize that God works in and with all our choices. The good choices and the bad calls. Looking up means we know we have the ultimate parenting partner on our side. And we find freedom in the knowledge that he is ready to deal with our imperfections and ready to implement his perfect plan if we will only let him help.

Looking out means we pull our gaze off the here and now to view the long-term goal. Plant our vision on the end result so that it fuels us through the pains and perils of immediate life. Looking out means we see why short-term frustrations can lead to long-term gains. It means we allow the horizon to grant us balance, direction, and the patience we need to get through today.

Where we look has a huge effect on where we're headed. Let's make sure we are looking in places that help, not hinder, us.

Challenge 1:
We Fear We'll Make a Bad Choice
The Major Moral Sneaky Toy Incident

Every mother has had those moments when something deep inside you says, "This is important—this is a crucial moment here—pay close attention." They don't come as much when your children are babies, but as they grow older, those hinge-pin moments come more frequently. If we're looking down, recognizing the altitude of our parenting, we'll put down the vacuum or the newspaper or the telephone and zero in on those moments. The most precious moments I've known as a mother have often been about stopping something "important" I was doing to zero in on a *truly* important moment with my child.

Let me share an example from a recent mistake my son made. CJ took a brand new toy to school, eager to show it off to his friends, and lost it. A perfectly common, perfectly normal incident for a seven-year-old-boy. Not really a major moral dilemma. You'd think.

CJ was understandably upset. Losing a new toy is one of a little life's great tragedies. I would soon discover, though, that there were much larger lessons in it for both of us.

First of all, I noticed a detail that triggered some questions, which is how I found out about the whole incident in the first place. The toy had several parts, and I noticed only one of them was in his backpack when he came home from school. I wasn't looking for it, but I was looking enough to notice it. Do you catch the difference?

As we discussed the situation, details revealed to me that CJ had purposely tucked the toy in his backpack *out of my*

231

sight because he was afraid I'd say he couldn't take it to school. Right here is where I needed to *look down*. The real issue here, the real problem, was not the lost toy. It was his trying to slip it in under the radar and take it to school. In fact, I would have told him he *could* take it to school because I understand the joy of new toys. I'm the first person to drive to a friend's house and show off a new possession because I believe joy is worth sharing—even if it's just a cool new set of knitting needles and you don't even knit. But I would have insisted he put his name on the toy first. And because he didn't, it was lost for days.

I was looking down enough to see that the true issue here was defiance and, for lack of a better word, sneakiness. I was also looking down enough to see this for the bud of the major issue it was. Sure, it was a small incident, but it was also our first episode of a major moral lesson.

We came down quite hard on poor little CJ. And as I watched that heartbreaking, quivering lower lip, my heart ached at his misery, and a tiny voice inside me was saying, "Don't be so hard on him. It was just a toy. Are you sure you're not overreacting?"

Dr. E. Maurlea Babb proposes that wisdom is the ability to have such an inner dialogue and know which voice should prevail. I agree. I'd add, though, that the ability to know which voice ought to prevail comes from a willingness to *look down*. To look at the real neglect to CJ if we *hadn't* come down hard on him. Lost toys are one thing; the consequences of deception are quite another.

Yes, I feared we'd been unduly hard on CJ. I feared we might have made a bad call in the delicate balance of mercy and discipline. I wondered if and when we'd catch the next deception—or how many previous ones we'd missed. But I also felt we made the wisest choice as parents. Mostly because we chose to *make a choice* as parents.

Was it scary and hard? Yes. But the courage of looking down isn't removing fear, and it isn't pretending that by making such choices we don't run the risk of making the wrong choice. The courage of looking down is *facing* those odds and acting.

Sneaking a toy to school is the most basic of examples. The older my children get, the less black and white the tough choices of parenting will be. Instead of choosing between two options, I'll find myself choosing between ten options with twenty outcomes. Not to mention I'll soon need to figure out how much of each choice is mine to make. My fear over Amanda's bad choices can't ignore that they are increasingly her bad choices to make. I must remind myself, however, of the good choices that can be made. I must also remind myself that in many instances the worst possible choice is *not to choose at all.*

So many variables fly in our faces. How are we to calm our fears over which to choose? Parenting is also about *looking up.* It is about trusting God to help us make such tough choices and to be sovereign over the ramifications of our choice. How easily we forget that God is big enough to work with any choice we make. Of course we often frustrate his intent by not making the best choice or by not asking for his wisdom and guidance, but we never prevent God from working.

God is our Father, and we're not exactly model children. He knows the perils of parenting. Think God can't understand the agony of punishing children for wrongdoing, the second-guessing of involved parenting? Remember Adam and Eve? Near as I can tell, they were the only children who were really, truly, "grounded for life." Remember Israel wandering and whining in the desert for forty years? Talk about a long "time out"! And then there was King David— the preeminent good kid gone bad.

God is the ultimate parent, which makes him the ultimate parenting partner. Our God not only understands what we're going through, but he's willing to participate. He's willing—even eager—to put his power into your parenting. The God who accomplished something as death-defying and illogical as parting the Red Sea is your ultimate parenting partner when facing serious illness, danger, or daunting finances. The God who saved Daniel from the fiery furnace, when a king was ready to toast him for insubordination, can protect your child from the class bully.

It doesn't require a crisis of epic proportions; your heavenly Father is interested in every aspect of your parenting. I have prayed over playdates, finding birthday presents, potty training, mean teachers, math tests, finding lost stuffed animals, parking spaces, summer camps, and Happy Meal toys. I have found that the more I call God into my parenting, the more I sense his presence in my parenting. Who of us can't use a stronger sense of divine guidance on this rocky road of raising children?

> *Our God not only understands what we're going through, but he's willing to participate. He's willing—even eager—to put his power into your parenting.*

You may find yourself afraid, staring into the abyss of a parenting challenge you do not think you can handle. You may find yourself facing a dozen serious options with no clear choice. You may find yourself simply at the very end of your resources.

Stop and look up. Ask God for strength. Remind yourself of his power and wisdom and that those things are right beside you, ready to help you at that very moment. Call to mind a few victories. Call to mind the attributes of our powerful and loving Lord. Grab a piece of paper and list ten things you do well as a parent—and do not let yourself stop at six. Know that it is no accident you find yourself in this particular situation with this particular child.

Then gather your courage so you can look down and see what's truly at stake. Have the courage to call a crucial moment for what it is.

And remember mercy.

God is no heartless tyrant, and parenting is not an all-or-nothing proposition. If you miss one of those crucial teachable moments, I believe you've missed *an* opportunity—not *the* opportunity but *an* opportunity. Like those silly VeggieTales sang in *Jonah*, "Our God is a God of second chances." And third chances. And fourth, and

> If you miss one of those crucial teachable moments, I believe you've missed an opportunity—not the opportunity but an opportunity.

fifth, and as many as it takes. Look down at the loss of the missed opportunity, but don't forget to look up at the grace of knowing another opportunity will come soon. It's nothing God can't handle. He knows just how to work with the place you're in. He'll compensate in his perfect wisdom, and you'll grow from the experience as well.

Fear-Facing Questions

Can you name a situation in your parenting right now in which an issue is really much bigger than the problem at hand—in which one act was really a hint at a much larger issue? Are you pleased with how you're handling the situation? What might you change to improve it?

Fear Fighter

Look at a fearful situation both directions:

1. *Look down.* What's truly at stake? What's the big picture issue?
2. *Look up.* How can God help me? How can I trust him to work with whatever decision I make?

Like looking both ways before you cross the street, looking up and down before you make a decision helps reduce your fear and enables you to act wisely.

Faith-Finding Verse

Surely God is my salvation; I will trust and not be afraid. The Lord, the Lord, is my strength and my song; he has become my salvation.

Isaiah 12:2

Challenge 2:
Fear Blinds Us to the Bigger Picture

Why Parenthood Is the Only Place "I Hate You!"
Is a Compliment

Looking down will make it impossible for you to cross a tightrope. Staring at your feet robs you of viewing the horizon, which is crucial to your sense of balance. It's why it is hard to stand on one foot with your eyes closed—you need vision to help keep you upright.

It matters, then, where you plant your focus. My tightrope teacher informed me that the best place to plant my focus was "out"—to the place where I wanted to end up. Simply put, the view that was going to get me to the other side was the view *of* the other side, fixing my eyes on the place where the wire met the opposite platform.

Parenting shares the same principle. Our view of the end goal, of the long-term results of any given situation, will be what gets us where we want to go. Let me share a practical example of how *looking out* helps us through a parenting challenge.

If you have not had the gut-wrenching experience of having your child yell, "I hate you!" to your face, know that it is one of the worst benchmarks of motherhood. However universal, however unavoidable, it is still awful. Knowing it is surely coming will do nothing to soften the gut punch of its arrival. It hurts to hear. And if you would like an invitation to fear the quality of your parenting, this incident is one of motherhood's finest.

I tried not to crumble when Mandy yelled it at me from behind her bedroom door. I think she was in kindergarten.

I tried to be calm and to keep some perspective. I failed miserably. I eventually got to the place where I could absorb that emotion, not back away from her, and recognize her lashing out as the cry for love that it was. But it took a long, weepy half-hour during which both of us were just plain miserable.

The reason this is an important benchmark in your child's development is that she will only yell, "I hate you!" when she knows it will not drive you away. When she recognizes that your relationship is permanent, beyond anything she might be feeling at the time. When she has overcome the very basic fear that you might leave her. Only then can she learn that you are two different people, and that different people have different needs and wants.

I don't claim it was fun or easy or that knowing any of what I've written above would have given me a shred of comfort during that horrible half-hour. But looking long term, I could take a deep breath, get a glimpse of the bigger picture, and know that Mandy's ability to voice an emotion, being secure enough to lash out, and learning to disagree were important steps on her journey.

And oh, how we need the bigger picture as mothers. Motherhood is chock full of potshots like "I hate you." Growing up is hard work. We cushion a lot of blows, absorb a lot of blowups, and continually cut some slack for our children. Not to mention the pure logistics of keeping a household together. If we focus on the daily drudgery that is childrearing, we'll lose our motivation in a week.

A week? Some days all it takes is an afternoon. Those are the days when we have to especially focus on the long-term goal of launching wonderful, contributing members of the human race so we can gain fuel for the journey.

It is tough to keep one foot in the long term. We are by our nature creatures of the here and now. That is why delayed gratification is perhaps the most difficult value to learn. We live in the age of the microwave—the instant life. We want to get thin now, smart now, rich now, happy now. We're far more allured by the claim to "lose thirty pounds in thirty days" than "do this and you'll gain a healthy body weight in two years." But, like every dieting veteran knows, it is the two-year plan that is more likely to be not only successful but lasting.

We want happy, healthy kids now. We don't want to wrestle with eleven time-outs this afternoon, and we really detest the particular torture of staying home with a grounded child. It is infinitely easier to let the infraction slide because we need to get to the store this afternoon than it is to call the error, inflict the punishment, and then lock ourselves in the house for the rest of the day with a teenager in a foul mood.

If we keep our focus on the peril of the present day— pacifier battles, sleepless nights, algebra, diapers, dance recital hysterics, S.A.T. scores—it won't take long for fear to overtake us. But if we pull our eyes forward, toward the horizon of where we're headed, then we let the goal pull us toward itself.

Sure, it's slow going. Ever see anybody run on a tightrope?

Fear-Facing Questions

What daily battle feels beyond your ability to cope right now? Can you see the long-term value in it? Why or why not? How will the answer help you conquer your fear and frustration?

Fear Fighter

Find yourself a horizon. Look to the long-term applications of any current problem or fear. How will the current struggle help you and your child develop a year from now? Three years from now? Ten years from now? Call upon the help of seasoned parents and other mentors to give you the perspective that keeps you headed in the right direction.

Faith-Finding Verse

Not that I have already . . . been made perfect, but I press on to take hold of that for which Christ Jesus took hold of me. Brothers, I do not consider myself yet to have taken hold of it. But one thing I do: Forgetting what is behind and straining toward what is ahead, I press on toward the goal to win the prize for which God has called me heavenward in Christ Jesus.

Philippians 3:12–14

Challenge 3:
Fear Distorts Our View;
Our View Distorts Our Fear

Looking at the World through Hormone-Colored Glasses

On good days, most moms make good choices. They're not all good days, though, are they?

Bad days are another thing altogether. There are days—*way* to many of them—when I'm so overwhelmed by life that I don't want to catch the seeds of a major moral issue. The only thing I want to catch is the next bus out of town.

What happens then? No wise parenting choices. I overreact. I let stuff slide that I shouldn't. You name it. That's why it's also important to know that looks can be deceiving and perception is relative.

Getting our view altered for the better doesn't seem to happen often in life. No, life seems ready to hand us ways to alter our view for the worse. To distort it.

How can our view become distorted? Let's talk hormones, shall we? Catch me at the right time of the month, and I can convince you the world is coming to an end. Every nuance is a portent of doom. The offhand remark I would have dismissed a week ago now festers in my gut. Name an issue and I'll find a way to blow it out of proportion. That's not to say that the issue at hand isn't really there—it most likely is. It's my *view* of the problem that is whacked out on hormones.

Sure, I wish it were different. Everyone in my *household* wishes it were different. But this is one place where wishing just won't make it so. Hormone fluctuations are a fact of life for our half of the species. To fail to recognize the

> Not only have you lost the ability to have an inner dialogue and know which voice should prevail, but the conflicting little voices in your head aren't even a dialogue — they're a gang fight!

power it wields over my perspective, to pretend that I'm seeing as clearly as I was before my estrogen levels played havoc with my viewpoint, would be just plain dumb.

The hormones, unfortunately, are not the only thing that distorts my view. I have come to recognize several influences that skew my vision when it comes to parenting crises. For me, and I'm guessing for nearly every mother on the planet, sleep deprivation can be a venerable foe. Like spiking hormones, lack of sleep can allow me to take a small issue and lather it up into a life-threatening crisis. Remember my newborn son's test results—the ones that sent me into a tizzy of imagining life with a mentally challenged child? It wasn't just the crisis nature of my household that made such a moment possible, it was also the fact that I hadn't had five consecutive hours of sleep in over two weeks. Remember that crises often breed lack of sleep, and you end up with a nasty emotional brew.

A knee-jerk decision or reaction can be regrettable when you don't have a clear picture of the situation. Not only have you lost the ability to have an inner dialogue and know which voice should prevail, but the conflicting little voices in your head aren't even a dialogue—they're a gang fight!

When your life is distorted—be it by hormones, lack of sleep, or whatever—it's important to realize you can't always trust your view. When something looks bad, take a moment to see if you've got a clear picture. Can you see the multiple sides of the situation? Can you identify the advantages and disadvantages of the choices available to you? Are you even *seeing* all your choices? You might be completely on track in your assessment, but you might not be, and it would be wise to deal with that truth first.

One of the hardest things in parenting is to know when you've lost your cool. Situations often conspire to overwhelm us. If we can't see clearly enough to cope, how on earth are we going to have enough wits about us to know we can't see clearly? Should we sit around waiting for parenting to give us a break so we can catch our breath and clear our heads? Well it would be nice if that could happen, but I don't think I'll catch a real break for about eighteen years. So how do we parents see the edge clearly enough to know we've gone over it? I haven't really found the total answer to this problem yet, but I have a few coping strategies that I'll pass on to you.

First, if you're the kind of woman whose hormones have a field day with her composure, recognize those mood swings for the powerful forces they are. And—here's the important part—don't count on your finely tuned sense of self-control to let you know it. At the right time of the month, I don't possess even one atom of self-control. I'm lucky I'm being civil and speaking in complete sentences. I can't count on me; I need something more concrete.

What works for me is a calendar. I took one of those small calendars the banks invariably send every January and pasted it to the inside of my bathroom cabinet. I tucked a pencil on the cabinet shelf. I marked down when my cycles fell and when I predicted the next one would fall. I get as nasty when I ovulate as I do during PMS (and oh, isn't that fun?), so I mark down the approximate ovulation date as well. Why? Because when my world looks black and I'm sure the kids will never make it to college and my house will never be clean *ever, ever again,* I can look at that calendar. That calendar never lies. The pure facts of those dates tell me that at least *a part* of what's going on has nothing to do with the situation outside my body but a good deal to do with what's going on inside my body.

Am I saying this little calendar makes everything better? Not in the least. Some days it just means I'm flying off the handle *knowing full well* I'm flying off the handle (which has yet to *stop* me from flying off the handle, but I'm working on it). It means I stand a chance of catching myself before I make a major decision or choice based on what I'm feeling that week because I've learned that there's a good possibility the world will look rather different the next week. If I were really thorough, I'd write in red, "MAKE NO MAJOR DECISIONS RIGHT NOW," across those days. Perhaps I ought to snag my husband's calendar and write, "DON'T LET ALLIE DO ANYTHING RASH," as well. Or maybe, "MOUNT ALLIE'S GONNA BLOW. GET OUTTA TOWN," would be more appropriate. You get the picture.

I know the above sounds rather silly, but there is some value to giving my family fair warning. Not that it excuses my bad behavior, but it lets everyone know it's harder for Mom to keep an even keel right now. Some days there ought to be an air raid siren in my kitchen. What we do have is a funny little sign called "Mom's Mood-o-Meter" that has a wooden heart you move between five small pegs labeled "Super," "Good," "O.K.," "Bad," and "Watch Out." Somehow the idiocy of moving that wooden heart makes it easier to cope. And yes, I admit there have been times when I've caught my kids moving that heart down to "Watch Out" even before I realize I've become nasty. Talk about being humbled at a time when I'm not exactly itching for personal growth.

The same can be said of when I've not been getting enough sleep, when family members are sick, or when I am sick. Those are the days when parenting's fears pull me under. I become convinced I'm giving my kids a lifetime set of "issues" rather than a lifetime set of memories. That little calendar and that silly Mood-o-Meter remind me that this too shall pass.

I ought to stop here and talk about when this does *not* pass. There will come a time in almost every one of our lives when it is appropriate and wise to seek professional help. Stress, depression, and chemical imbalances are serious issues and should not be taken lightly. There is a very important distinction between just having a bad time of it and suffering from clinical depression.

The societal stigma of seeking mental health assistance is going away, but it hasn't gone completely. America's veneration of the strong and independent makes it hard to admit we are the weak and frail beings we are. Millions of women suffer needlessly from clinical depression, anxiety attacks, and panic disorders simply because they do not understand the nature of their illness. It is sad that the very symptoms of those illnesses often cloud a woman's ability to seek help. It is difficult to go see a doctor if your anxiety is so powerful it will not allow you to leave your home.

Here is where *looking down* can be useful. If you wish to be a healthy, effective mother to your children, you must recognize the taxing nature of motherhood and its capacity to wear you down. To understand the difficulty and importance of our job is also to accept its costs and demands.

> If you wish to be a healthy, effective mother to your children, you must recognize the taxing nature of motherhood and its capacity to wear you down.

I find it helpful to think of it in athletic terms. No one enters a marathon without training—you'd virtually ensure your failure. No, you'd first make sure you had the support, stamina, nutrition, and strength to undertake such a huge challenge. In the same vein, no athlete would undertake an Olympic competition without first tending to an injury—either getting it resolved or getting extra support for the weakened limb. It's a matter of respect for the job at hand.

Motherhood is the "mother of all marathons," wouldn't you say? Your tasks are just as emotionally demanding as an athlete's tasks are physically demanding. You must show the same respect for the job at hand. If you have an inkling that something is seriously wrong with either you or your children, this is no time to let fear's paralysis or denial win. Find the courage to admit there might be a problem. Stare down the altitude of parenting and know what it may cost you if you don't get it checked out. Do not allow yourself to fall into fear's trap of doing nothing. Your troubles will not go away if you try not to look at them. If it is something within the natural ups and down of human life, a mental health professional can reassure you. If it is something that requires attention, that professional can get you to the help you or your children need.

Dr. Paulette Toburen offered these instances when she would advise seeking professional help:

- If your fear is rendering you unable to function in other areas of your life such as sleep, appetite, sex drive, ability to concentrate, wanting to be with friends, etc.
- If you grow to fear the fear—i.e., if you experience not only the panic itself but live in fear of the next wave of panic.
- If you feel out of control for a long period of time.
- If you feel like it will never blow over or if you feel hopeless.

If the concept of seeing a mental health professional is simply too much for you, start with something closer to home such as your medical doctor, a good friend, or your pastor. I guarantee you will not invite their scorn for admitting your feelings—you will win their admiration. It takes courage and strength to face up to the possibility of a problem. But you cannot fix it if you will not look at it.

Fear-Facing Questions

What may be playing havoc with your perception right now? Are there things like hormones or lack of sleep distorting your view of a particular problem? How would recognizing that influence change your immediate reaction? Is waiting or talking to someone else a valuable choice?

Fear Fighter

Know your obstacles. Use a calendar in your medicine cabinet to chart your roller-coaster hormones. Log your diet or sleep patterns if you think they may be skewing your perceptions. If this month's tight financial situation sends you into the stratosphere, let your family budget show you things aren't bad when you take the full year into consideration. Use whatever hard facts you can find to fight your distorted view. Do not be frightened into inactivity if those indicators tell you professional help may be needed. The demands of your job are too great not to get the help you need.

Faith-Finding Verse

Yet if you devote your heart to him and stretch out your hands to him ... you will lift up your face without shame; you will stand firm and without fear. You will surely forget your trouble, recalling it only as waters gone by. ... You will be secure, because there is hope; you will look about you and take your rest in safety.

Job 11:13, 15–16, 18

Hey, I Can See My Child from Up Here!

Where are you looking? Where is your gaze fixed as a mother? Is it a place that helps your balance and focus or a place more likely to skew the view? The Empire State Building grew no shorter, no taller, nor more dangerous during my time there—only the direction of my gaze changed. The eyes aren't the windows of the soul for nothing.

Sometimes, I find myself looking *out* for all the wrong reasons. I'm not looking at my goal or horizon but looking at everyone else. The moms who seem like they have it so much more together. The ones with clean homes, whose kids behave well in public, who iron their kids' clothes and bake birthday cakes instead of picking one up from the supermarket. I can't be one of them—it's not in me. I forget I have other gifts and worry instead that I'm failing my children in some crucial area. Then up creeps the fear. Comparison seems such an eager midwife to fear and worry.

Hormones and sleep deprivation may surely skew our vision, but insecurity is just as capable of distorting our view. How easily we think, "If I were a good mother I would ..." instead of the more truthful statement, "If I were *that* mother I would ..." For then we would remember that we are not *that* mother, we are *this* mother. Then we would see ourselves as God sees us—just the right gal for the job.

Comparison skews our view of our children as well. For that reason, I would add *look at* to our list of *look up, look down,* and *look out.* When I allow comparison a foothold in my mothering, I begin to second-guess why my daughter does not possess a certain strength another girl has or why my son can't seem to do what another boy does easily. When I let my expectations or desires for my children color my view too completely, I do not truly see *them*. If I take the time and focus to look at them, *really* look at them, behold them for the unique masterpieces they are, my worry turns to wonder. I see them for who they are, not for how they stack up.

Which of us hasn't wanted, yearned, longed to be seen for *who we are*, not how we stack up? Perfect love would see us for who we are and all we can be. Such love could not help but offer us courage. It is why the Bible tells us "perfect love drives out fear" (1 John 4:18).

I've said it before and it bears repeating: If love is the answer—and it is—then moms have got what it takes.

Come, ladies, we're almost across. Time to head for the grandest of finales.

Chapter 10

THE FINALE

"I get anxious about everything that isn't getting done. I'm going to miss something important; I just know it."

"I fear my child will turn out just like me."

"I fear other people will see me as a failure if my kids are not perfect all the time."

"I fear what will happen when my kids find out that they're smarter than me."

What's Worth All This Risk?

We're here.

We've come across the abyss to touch a grateful toe on the platform on the other side. We turn and stand in awe of what we've just done. We look out and wave to the audience, basking in the applause of a daring job well done. The finale is what we're all shooting for, isn't it? Maybe. Come along with me, first. I have some things I want to show you.

I want to tell you about The Box. It is an ordinary container, bearing slips of paper—cards, actually. The ones I told you about in the first pages of this book.

I keep The Box in my dining room because it is safer to have it there. If I had the cards in the tiny corner of my basement I call my office (a gross overstatement, I assure you) or anywhere near where I write, it would be much harder. I prefer to keep them safely contained in The Box. The one time I spread the hundreds of cards on the dining room table, like the wide-open ocean of emotion they are, it was devastating. I couldn't look at it. I felt it was too much to bear—a height with too deadly a fall. I never did it again—opting to look at them instead in sections, piles, sorted stacks, but never the overwhelming whole that they are.

Why? Because the parent in me wants to "make it all better." I want to write the book that will point a clear and compelling path to the peace we all crave. I want to have the answer. I want to be a worthy helper. But The Box seems enormous, filled with more troubles than I want to face.

I do not think of myself as a very fearful woman. I know many, many, *way too many* women, though, who are fearful. It seemed to me that everyone around me was more frightened than I, and I wrote this book as much to figure out how I had escaped that fear as to offer a path to courage. God's call to write this book came so clearly, so strongly, so surprisingly that I could not ignore it, even though I felt unqualified to write it.

When I began to unearth the strength and depth of pain women were feeling on the topic, I felt even more unqualified. You are too precious to place in the hands of this pretender. Like Moses, I kept arguing with God that *surely* there was another person more suited to the task.

Those stacks and stacks of cards cried out, *this needs to be done right*. There is so much need. So much pain. Too much at stake. So many women begging for the courage I think I have but don't know how I got.

This wire was too high for me to walk. Surely there was another person, another more suitable mother, a therapist with more knowledge, a woman with more experience and compassion for fear than I. Surely God could select a better candidate to write this book. I'm just a forty-year-old ex–theater major, ex-fundraiser turned housewife who can string a pretty sentence. I rush entirely too quickly to food for comfort. I overreact on a regular basis. I cannot lead God's precious daughters to courage.

And suddenly, I *became* that very fearful mother, thinking that I could not be the guide that you deserve. I stare at these chapters and think that surely I have missed some important topic, botched some vital strategy, failed you somehow. I fear that somehow you will see through my clever turn of phrase to the frightening truth that I am only a mother, not an expert. I am certain you will see that my humble efforts could never, ever meet the huge need I see in those cards. And I know a fear so deep it took me *months* to admit it.

Why write a book on fear? Why try to fight it? Why do all the hard work of meeting fear with courage? Why me?

Why? Because I—and you—need courage, whether it is to write, to mother, to serve, or to do anything. Courage to bring all of ourselves—every gift and every shortcoming—to this task of motherhood, to this task of life. Courage to love, to risk, to grow. The courage to demand faith's transformation of us, of our world. Courage to take God up on his astounding offer of grace in order to change the world—one young soul at a time.

> *Courage to bring all of ourselves—every gift and every shortcoming—to this task of motherhood.*

Oh, I wanted to walk away from this task. This book has been pulled out of me kicking and biting and fighting every inch of the way. I procrastinated in ways I never imagined. I even went to the *hardware* store. Even my husband recognized that speeding off to the coffee shop was one thing, but procrastinating at the hardware store meant I was *really* desperate to run away from this. And you know how I felt, because each of us has at some time yearned for a way to run away from the overwhelming task of motherhood.

So how did I write this? One truth, one thought enabled me to stare all my fears and doubts in the face and muster the courage to meet the task. I have been called. Me—with every gift and every inadequacy.

You have been called as well. You have been given a precious, perfect calling. The Lord Almighty, maker of heaven and earth, God of things seen and unseen, chose *you* to raise your children. Not by worth or skill or any favorable qualities. In fact, I believe God calls us to tasks *because* of our faults. The flaws you have—the flaws we all have—do not diminish the perfection of this call. The flaws—the doubts, the fears, the mistakes, the worries—are, in fact, part of the perfection of this call.

The courage we seek is not a gift. Faith is a gift, but courage is a hard-won prize, a weapon crafted by gut-wrenching effort. A sword honed by faith and wielded in strength against a formidable enemy.

Our fears are real: a powerful darkness, an ever-present threat. But it is not right that fear should win. Joy is waiting to claim the victory. The world becomes a good and joyful place—not a scary, dangerous place—when our hearts discover how to see it that way.

If you gain only one thing from this book, let it be that courage is a *choice*, an act of defiant will, a battle waged against fear. A battle to meet strength with strength, to find as much courage as there is fear.

I wish you could have stood with me in a tiny gym in Evanston, Illinois, as my foot hit the opposite side of the tightrope. As I made the best use I could of the tools and training available to me, and did the unthinkable. I walked a wire. Forty-year-old, unathletic, Mommy-shaped me walked a tightrope.

As I whooped in joy on the opposite side, on the *finale* side of the wire, I turned in astonishment, needing to see again that impossible gap I had just crossed. Suddenly I understood. I honored all the falling. I recognized the usefulness of the mistakes, began to see that it wasn't really the *getting across* that I prized but the fun and fascination I had in learning to do so. I understood, just for a moment, why it was that Philippe Petit did not want to leave his wire between the Twin Towers. It was because he had known what I just had discovered: It is the journey, the walking that matters, not the finale. The finale's really not a finale at all.

Now, with that knowledge in hand, I see my parenting journey differently. Just as I have come to learn that courage is its own reward, I am coming to learn that parenting is its own reward also. Sure, I seek to teach my children as I parent them. Now, though, I realize that God has just as much to teach *me* through parenting. The journey across this wire is as much for me as for them.

If you were hoping this book would teach you a way to make the fear go away, you will be disappointed. I have discovered no way to make fear disappear. I have come to learn, though, that courage is not about making fear go away. It is the force wielded in the face of fear.

> Just as I have come to learn that courage is its own reward, I am coming to learn that parenting is its own reward also.

The courage you seek is already inside you. The fierce love you bear for your children is the kindling that can set fire to courage. God has chosen you, created you, gifted you with the children in your family. There is no mistake in that selection.

There is no mistake in that selection.

God, your Creator and the Creator of your children, wishes *you* to raise these children. Knowing their faults, knowing their struggles, knowing their outcomes both good and awful, he has chosen you. He will partner with you, train you, protect you, guide you, and equip you to make it to the other side. I can envision him, standing on the *finale* platform, arms outstretched, knowing all this journey holds for you, anticipating its joyful result. Take him up on his invitation.

Surely your feet will hurt from the narrow tension of the wire. It is a supreme effort to keep your life in balance, to hold the heavy balancing pole. There are problems, distortions, stumbles up here on the wire. Hard training, brain-aching mental challenges, and acts of faith are needed to get across. This stuff is hard. Don't think for a moment that God doesn't already know that.

I'm here to tell you what you probably already know: Hard is worthwhile. To shepherd a human soul through life is hard. No mother would tell you, though, that it is not worth it. As you conquer your fears, you grow. As you risk, you gain new insights, new strengths. Each small victory of courage engenders a new call to a new strength. Each time you meet a fear head-on, you inch one step closer to the astounding woman God called you to be. Each time you deny fear the upper hand, you welcome heaven that much closer.

Do not seek to face fear to be a better mother. Seek to face fear to be a better woman. Reach out to the grace and guidance God offers not just because of your children but because of you. As you become the woman God intended you to be, you become the mother God intends for your children. The mother your children deserve. The mother you fear you cannot be.

Everything you need to be that woman lies in the hands of God, and he is just waiting to give it to you.

Come up.

Take heart.

Cross the wire.

All of heaven will applaud you as you do.

NOTES

1. Gavin deBecker, *The Gift of Fear* (New York: Random House, 1999), 30.
2. Franklin D. Roosevelt, First Inaugural Address, 4 March 1933.
3. David D. Burns, *The Feeling Good Handbook* (New York: William Morrow and Company, 1989), 81.
4. Ibid., 90.
5. DeBecker, *The Gift of Fear,* 10.
6. Ibid., 35.
7. Philippe Petit, *To Reach the Clouds: My High Wire Walk Between the Twin Towers* (New York: North Point Press, 2002), 45.
8. Gavin deBecker, *Protecting the Gift* (New York: Random House, 1999), 84.
9. Diane Eble, *Abundant Gifts* (Wheaton, IL: Tyndale, 1999), introduction.
10. John J. Pelizza, *12 Ways to Get UP & GO!* audiocassette, (North Chatham, NY: Pelizza & Associates, 1999).
11. Michael Sena, "Portable Peace and Quiet," *Hemispheres,* August 2003, 84.
12. Susan Shaughnessy, commenting on a quote by Mary Gordon, *Walking on Alligators,* (New York: Harper Collins, 1993), 17.
13. D. W. Winnicott, *The Child and the Family* (London: Tavistock Publishing, 1957).
14. Shaughnessy, *Walking on Alligators.*
15. Burns, *The Feeling Good Handbook,* 240.

LEADER'S GUIDE

Introduction

A discussion group for moms provides a wonderful opportunity for personal growth, friendship, and encouragement. Women in the profession of motherhood can struggle with isolation if they do not have regular networking opportunities. They can feel unappreciated without a pat on the back every once in a while. And they can lose vision if they are not reminded of the importance of the job they are doing. This leader's guide is designed to stimulate the building of relationships that will encourage, equip, and educate moms. Whether your group is a small group that meets in your living room, or a larger moms' group, or a MOPS group that meets in a church or community building, the most important aspect of gathering together is intentionally building relationships.

Preparing to Lead

First, pray for the women in your group and for God's guidance as you lead the group.

Take some time each week before the group meets to familiarize yourself with the discussion agenda. Make notes on additional questions you might present to the group. Create a list of items you need to remember to bring to the meeting. Consider creating a "study basket" specifically for keeping items you will need each week. Pens, highlighters, name tags, index cards, notebook paper, and your copy of the book would be basic essentials. When special items are needed for a specific week, just drop them in the basket and you'll be assured to remember them!

You'll notice that every discussion has four parts, each playing an important role in meaningful interaction with the content and in relationship building. Let's take a quick look at the purpose of each part.

Icebreaker

When your group first gets together each week, you will find it beneficial to start out with a lighthearted, get-to-know-you-better activity. Each mom has probably had a hectic time just getting to the group and she may be preoccupied with thoughts of child care, household chores that are going undone, or juggling this week's carpool responsibilities or extracurricular activities. The 10–15 minute Icebreaker is designed to focus everyone on the people around them and the topic at hand. It fosters relationships and builds a sense of camaraderie through laughing and sharing together.

When you finish up the Icebreaker time, open the discussion part of your meeting with prayer. Commit your time to the Lord and ask him to lead your discussion.

Dig Deep

The best moms' groups are not led by leaders who like to hear themselves talk, but rather by leaders who draw out the thoughts of others. The questions in Dig Deep are designed to facilitate discussion rather than teach a lesson and will probably take about 30–45 minutes.

Don't feel confined by the questions listed in the leader's guide. If you believe another line of questions better fits your group, adjust the discussion to fit your group's needs. You might also refer to the personal reflection questions at the end of each chapter for further ideas.

During the group's discussion time your job will be to draw out the women. You will most likely have some women who want to monopolize the discussion and some who hardly say a word on their own. To draw out the woman who is quieter, you may find it useful to ask her some questions specifically to help her join the discussion. When a group member has the habit of monopolizing conversations, keep the discussion moving by calling on other women immediately after you pose a question. If the group gets off the subject in their discussions, simply pull the focus back to the original question posed to get back on track.

Apply

The true benefit of reading this book and discussing it with others is not to simply absorb new information, but rather to experience positive changes in daily life. The Apply section is designed to stimulate personal application and provide the opportunity for the moms to share how they have been challenged or moved to action. Some participants may want to invite one another to hold them accountable to make the changes God is impressing upon them, or commit to encouraging one another through challenging change. Others may discover life-changing implications they would have never thought of on their own. This vitally important part of the discussion may take approximately 10–20 minutes to complete.

Pray

Prayer may be either invigorating or intimidating depending on a person's understanding and experience with prayer. If the moms in your group are comfortable praying together, take some time at the end of your group to pray together about the things you have learned. As the leader, take the responsibility of closing out the prayer time when the group seems to be finished praying or when the clock requires that you end your time together.

If your group is not comfortable praying together, then close the group in prayer yourself or ask another member of the group who is comfortable praying aloud to do so. The prayer suggestions are simply suggestions. Pray whatever God lays on your heart to pray. There is no right or wrong when it comes to prayer; simply talk to God as you would talk to a friend.

Assignments and Notes

In some chapters you may find an assignment for the next week or notes to help your planning. These will help you gather together any items that might be needed in the next chapter or the coming weeks.

It is a core value of Hearts at Home to provide resources to moms, moms' groups, and moms' group leaders. We hope this book provides you the opportunity to interact with women who are doing the same job you are doing. Our goal is that this, and other Hearts at Home resources, will encourage, educate, and equip women in the profession of motherhood!

Jill Savage
Author of *Professionalizing Motherhood*
Founder and Director, Hearts at Home

Chapter 1: The High-Wire Walk of Parenting

Icebreaker

Have the moms share what they feel is their favorite unproductive coping strategy for fear. Is it food? Shopping? Something else? Share your own first to help everyone overcome any embarrassment. You'll probably all end up laughing at how similarly women react to fear (can you say "chocolate"?).

Dig Deep

1. Have the women share whatever they are comfortable with regarding the security of their childhood. How do they feel it has colored their parenting? Where has it been positive? Where has it brought negative impulses?

2. What is courage to you? Where do you feel you need more courage in your parenting? Have the women share examples of courage that they admire—from present day to Bible heroes—and tell why they admire them.

3. Explore the caution we all feel as mothers. Can the women remember a time when caution crossed the line into smothering—either in their parenting or in their childhood? What would they change if they could face

the situation all over again? What would they repeat? Has anything been learned in the experience?

Apply

1. On a chalkboard or large piece of paper, have the women make a group list of their natural responses to fearful situations. If you need to jump-start the discussion, use an example such as a child missing in the grocery store. Don't edit; just list every response that is mentioned. Then see if you can classify the responses into ones that are survival/instinct-based, ones that are wise and methodical, and ones that are silly and reactionary. Choose the three you think would be most productive in solving the situation.

2. Have the women share about a time when they felt their child was threatened. What was their response? Did the aggressiveness of their own actions surprise them or disturb them? What did they learn about themselves from the experience?

3. Take some time to begin exploring fear's positive uses. How does fear prepare us for threatening situations?

What does the presence of fear mean? Why is it that fear is one of the best producers of results? See if each woman can identify a situation in which she experienced fear but grew stronger as a result.

Pray

Take some time to thank God for the precious gift of your children. Pray for each child by name. Hold up their gifts, their challenges, and any special situations that need to be covered in prayer.

Pray for mothers in true danger today. Pray that women raising children in the midst of war and rampant disease will know God's peace and compassion. Pray for mothers of children in military service and emergency rescue situations—the men and women who risk their lives daily for the sake of others.

Pray that God will bless the time you spend in this study. Ask him to show you all he has planned for you to learn, and request that your heart be open to his teaching.

Chapter Two: The Platform

Icebreaker

Have the women complete the following sentences:

(From husband) "You're just like your mother when

_____."

(From children) "You're just like Grandma when

_____."

(From self) "I'm just like my mother when

_____."

Many of the women will come up with negative comparisons at first. Next, see if you can encourage them to come up with positive comparisons.

Dig Deep

1. Discuss the concept of "baggage." What baggage do the women feel they've brought into their marriage? Into their mothering? We usually think of baggage as bad. Is there anything good about it?

2. Talk about Allie's "Oreo dilemma." What issues have that kind of emotional charge for each of the women? Are there universal ones? Are there unique ones drawn from personality?

3. What were each woman's initial parenting fears? If there are new moms in the group, what are their "novice parent" fears? Can other women in the group offer the encouragement of "I've been there"? Are there fears

every mother faces? How can knowing every mother faces them help to encourage us?

Apply

1. Have each woman rate herself for risk tolerance on a scale of one to ten. Now have her rate her husband and children. If you'd like, extend the exercise to include how she would rate her parents and in-laws. What patterns do you see? Where are there conflicts? Can you draw any conclusions about relationships from them?

2. Have each woman identify a fear she is currently experiencing. Don't look for solutions just yet; simply examine the fear. How does her risk tolerance help the situation? Where does it hinder? Can she see any baggage playing a role in her reaction? Is this a fear in which logical solutions will help or not?

3. Take some time and do the "stick figure" exercise. Encourage each woman to do it at least three times, either asking the same question or related questions.

What have they learned? Was it what they expected, or are they surprised by what "paper mama" told them?

Pray
Ask God for the wisdom and vision to see each child's individual risk tolerance. Read Psalm 139 and thank God for the individual, perfectly created personality of each child. Thank God for his individual, perfect creation of each woman and her own risk tolerance.

Invite the women to share their current fears and pray for each situation. It might be a good idea to make praying over current fears a regular part of each time you meet. Make sure you share any results you see.

Chapter Three: The Wire

Icebreaker
Use a computer to make a set of "It's God's problem" stickers for each woman, or buy some sticker sheets and have the women make their own. Pass them out, and ask each woman to name one thing she'd love to put that sticker on today. Commit to sharing where those stickers ended up at the next meeting.

Dig Deep
1. Discuss how parenting often places us "between a rock and a hard place." Where does each of the women feel that both choices are undesirable? How do they perceive

those situations? How do they find they react to their lack of choice? Are they happy with those reactions?

2. In contrast, where do they feel good about themselves as parents? What glimpses of the good are energizing them these days? Encourage the women to share positives about each other as well. Give the moms a chance to get some of that much-needed affirmation!

3. Have any of the women shared Allie's experience of having God speak to her through her children? What was it like? What was the message? How did she know—or did she "just know"? If the mothers are all new moms with infants, find some older parent who can share her story as inspiration—or share your own.

Apply

1. As a group, rewrite Isaiah 43:1–7 for mothers. What would you put in place of "waters," "rivers," and "fires"? Why would it be important not to change a word of the first part of verse 4 but adapt the second

part? What will God bring to you in verses 6–7? Type up your revised verses and distribute them at the next meeting.

2. The only way over the bridge was over the bridge. Talk about what other parts of mothering, like the bridge, have only one solution. Then look at what kinds of people would be best to "drive the moms over the bridge." Let each mom think of three or four problems she's facing, then identify who might be a good person to offer support. Have each mom commit to calling on at least one of those resources before the next meeting.

3. Have each woman privately make a list of her circle of friends. Let her look over the list and identify which of them make good rescue parties. Which are more wisely called when the crisis is over? Is her best friend the person to call first? (Remind her that "no" is an acceptable answer.) Does she need to make some more friends with warrior souls?

Pray

Pray together the verses you rewrote of Isaiah 43. Thank God for his promise to stand by us in times of strife. Give the women an opportunity to lift up specific challenges they are facing.

Pray for the women's friendships. Ask that God send friends to those in need, give us the vulnerability to reach out for help, and provide the compassion to be there for others. Pray for women who feel friendless, such as those who've just moved to a new town, those who experience hatred or discrimination, or those who are far away from loved ones.

Spend some time in thanksgiving for the families represented in the group. Pray for the particular pairing of personalities, the ways husbands and wives can complement each other in parenting, the unique combination of children in each home. Ask for eyes to see the harmony as well as the conflict.

Chapter Four: The Altitude

Icebreaker

Have the women share what body part of their baby they most worried about. Was there a procedure they were always sure they would botch? Was it baths or baby Tylenol that made—or still makes—them most nervous?

Dig Deep

1. Discuss the two statements, "More fear doesn't automatically equal more danger. It only means more fear," and, "The actual dangers to our immediate family are, for the

most part, perceived." Would you agree or disagree? How should or shouldn't it affect your daily parenting?

2. Read Luke 12:1–11. These are big, serious ideas to contemplate. For what "yeast" do we need to be on guard? Do these warnings focus on what you usually worry about as parents, or do they guide us to larger issues? What assurances can we get from verses 6 and 7? How do verses 8–11 apply not just in public witness but in how we spiritually strengthen our children? Is there anything you need to ask the Holy Spirit to teach you to say at the time you should say it?

Apply

1. Ask the women to share stories of when they have endured significant pain or fear. You may need to keep a firm grasp on the conversation—once women get into labor stories they really get going. Make an effort to keep the stories brief and to the point. Are they all labor stories like Allie's? Has someone experienced the death of a close family member? What kind of courage have their experiences given each of these women? Have they stopped to recognize the strength of that survival? What happens to their own sense of courage when they do?

2. As a group, make a list of what you feel to be dangers to your children. Don't edit your answers; just make this a time of brainstorming because you need to identify both serious and silly fears. Now draw a line down the middle of a large piece of paper. Classify the fears you've listed. Which ones are real dangers? Which ones would you classify as only feeling dangerous? Would different women classify the same fear differently? Are there fears that are both? See what role individual perception plays in the strength of fear.

3. Look at the list you just made and pick three real dangers that seem to be the most common among your group. Assign research to each woman in the group: What local resources do you have to equip your children for these dangers? Are there local self-defense classes? Good books to read? Counselors who can offer good ways to get closer to teens? Police officers or rescue workers who can guide you? Work as a group to find good resources to rechannel your worry into preparation and prevention.

Pray

Pray over the mother-child relationship. Ask God to open up opportunities to deepen communication and for the words to speak. Thank him for his constant love and protection against true enemies.

Ask God for the ability to see clearly in a crisis. He can give us the eyes to see all there is to see when we're frightened by the height of our wire. Ask him to send us Joshuas in our lives who will remind us of the courage we've known in the past and encourage us in new challenges.

Ask God to increase our capacity to love and to give us strength and wisdom in our love. Ask him to help us to love when it is difficult or uncomfortable. Ask him to help us show a love to the world that will reflect God's marvelous love for us.

Chapter Five: The Balance Pole

Icebreaker

Have a balance contest. See who can stand on one leg the longest. Then try it with your eyes closed. For some truly relevant fun, give a box of Yodels (if you're lucky enough to live where you can get them) or Ho-Hos for a prize. Spend a little time in laughter as well. Bring in some funny mom-oriented comic strips, or just have a classic round of "stare down"—last one to crack a smile wins. At the very least, have every mom share—in just words or perhaps the real thing—her favorite "comfort junk food" (think of the potluck possibilities!).

Dig Deep

1. Talk about how parenthood is the constant process of readjustment. What new changes have caught the women most off guard recently? Are there strategies or subjects about which they have changed their minds over their parenting careers? Why or why not? Does this add flexibility to a mother, increase stress, or both?

2. Every mother has a possibility she dreads having to face. For Allie, it was a child with cognitive disabilities. What is it for each mother in your group? Assure them there are no judgmental voices here to condemn them—the answer is bound to be "politically incorrect," and we're talking about raw emotions, not thoughtful actions. Are there things the mothers have in common? What's unique? How does it affect the way we respond to parenting challenges?

3. Discuss why the bad things get our attention so easily. Talk about the obstacles to finding that silver lining in a crisis. Why does it take a conscious effort to seek out a solution or put a stop to worrying? What can we do to fight that natural tendency?

Apply

1. Read Proverbs 3:21–26. Talk about how sound judgment and discernment (v. 21), sleep (v. 24), and confidence (v. 26) can be the elements of a mother's balance. How can she call on those to create balance when "sudden disaster" (v. 25) strikes? On whom can she call? Where are good places to turn? Where are the bad ones?

2. Have each mother identify her "poles." What hobbies, activities, or friends uplift her? Have each mother list four of them. Now list what obstacles keep her from doing these enjoyable things on a regular basis. Have each mother pick one and share it with the group. Everyone can help brainstorm solutions for the obstacles, or you might even find something the whole group would enjoy and make plans to do it.

3. Challenge each mother to commit to try Gresko's technique of a fixed amount of time for fear and worry. Let each mother identify a current fear and choose the amount of time she wants to spend worrying about it each day next week. Hand out index cards and have the mothers write down the fear and its budgeted time. Ask her to sign it, like a contract, and place it on her bedroom mirror or someplace visible (depending upon the subject nature, more privacy may be called for). Have the women hold each other accountable for the coming week, and plan to share the results next time you meet.

Pray

Turn all the index cards face down on a table and pray over them. Ask God to honor each woman's commitment to a fixed amount of time, and ask him to send her perspective when she needs to move her attention elsewhere. Boldly ask for solutions to come to her and for God's peace to descend on her.

Thank God for being a source of joy. Ask him to send light and laughter into each woman's life during the coming week. Let each woman thank God for that person in her life who makes her laugh. Pray for women in such a state of crisis or mourning that laughter seems impossible, and ask God to send them comfort.

Chapter 6: Taking Steps

Note: The possibilities for practical learning here are too enticing to ignore. A request that everyone come to the meeting in their jammies is highly encouraged!

Icebreaker
Before your meeting, write out the instructions—step by step—for a diaper change. Be as specific as you can—as if the person reading the instructions has never done this before. Now, Mad-Lib style, remove several nouns, verbs, and adverbs. Without telling them the subject matter, let the women suggest nouns, verbs, and adverbs to fill in the blanks. Have a good laugh over the step-by-step instructions you have now!

Dig Deep
1. Have the women share times they were "frozen with fear." What snapped them out of it? What were the results of that immobility? Were there positive results? Negative results? Has it changed how they approach that situation or ones like it?

2. Discuss the risks our children need to take. How does fear hamper those growth opportunities? How much risk is too much? How do you know? Do you ever know?

3. Talk about illogical baby steps. Why do they work? Are logical ones better than silly ones? Why do you think it is that kinesthetic actions can help to snap us out of a fearful stupor?

Apply

1. Have each mother identify a fear or stress she is currently facing. What would "make it good"? What is possible to "make it better"? See if each woman can list some steps in the "better" direction to face her challenge. This is a good place for brainstorming and letting the women help each other come up with baby steps.

2. Have each woman make her own list of ten sense-based comforts. Encourage her to think about which sense has the most power for her and how she can capitalize on

that. Are there supplies she needs to have on hand so she can create these comforts? Would a daily or weekly dose of such comforts be beneficial?

3. Now have each woman make a similar list for other members of her family. What does she think would offer comfort to her husband on a stressful day? What about her toddler? How can she use this knowledge to create a haven of comfort in her home? What makes sense (pun intended) on a regular basis? What makes sense during times of crisis?

Pray

Today, pray on paper. Hand out sheets of paper, put on some quiet music, and read Psalm 116 out loud. Then let each woman write a private letter of prayer to God. End the meeting with the blessing from Psalm 116: "Be at rest once more, O my soul, for the LORD has been good to you" (v. 7).

Chapter 7: The Stumble

Icebreaker

Have each woman share an embarrassing moment from growing up. Fifth through eighth grade are particularly awkward times—what does each woman remember about those years? If you had to give it a supermarket tabloid style headline, what would it be? Laugh at how we goof up as we grow, even though it feels so painful at the time.

Dig Deep

1. Have the women discuss their parenting "battle scars." Are there things that happened to them when they were children that shapes how they parent today? What's an appropriate focus on how our parents have shaped us? Society is quick to blame parenting. What's good and bad about that trend?

2. What has been each woman's spectacular stumble to date? Do they feel comfortable sharing it (or perhaps just a part of it)? What has been the result of that experience? How can we get to a place of learning from it? How can we let it hamper us? What's to be gained from sharing the experience with other mothers? Are there some blunders that should never be shared?

3. Examine Allie's statement that "we don't own even 51 percent of the stock" in our children's outcome. How does that make each woman feel? Where's the freedom in it? Where's the fear? Do the women agree or disagree?

Apply

1. Have each woman draw a pie chart with three sections. Ask them to take a current parenting challenge and divide it into three parts: (1) those elements of the situation they can control, (2) those for which their children must take responsibility or for which personality is a factor, and (3) God's role in the situation. Does this help to focus their energies? When they do the chart for different children, what comes to light? Does it make things better or more confused?

2. Have the women list four current fears. Commit to praying about them at least three times before the next meeting. Make sure you leave time for sharing any results!

3. List the obstacles to a mother's social companionship. Why are they worth overcoming? What can be gained by a phone conversation? When do they need face-to-face companionship? Have each woman brainstorm three ideas for getting together with friends and implement one idea before the next meeting.

Pray

Pray for parents whose children have gone wrong. Ask God to give them the strength to continue loving, the courage to stand firm when needed, and the peace to know God is still in control. If you have a specific family in this situation, pray for them, but treat the situation with the sensitivity it deserves.

Ask God to remind us when we need to pray. We are so quick to seek to solve problems in our own strength. Request that God call each one of us to prayer as a first recourse instead of a last resort.

Pray that God will open up opportunities for companionship and fellowship for each woman in the group. Ask that he send solutions to the obstacles and that he bless the time women spend together. Ask for the sensitivity to know when to reach out to another mother and offer companionship. Thank him for the gift of friends.

Chapter 8: The Audience

Icebreaker

Have the women stand up. Place black, white, red, and blue (or any four colors) circles on the floor at each corner of the room. Call out the following statements and watch how the women divide up:

Your husband uttering the phrase, "You're being just like your mother," would lead you to:

kiss him—red circle

shoot him the dirtiest of looks—black circle

be distracted in wondering silence for the next twenty
   minutes—white circle

no reaction—blue circle

You have heard the phrase "I'll never do that to my
son/daughter"

from your son/daughter—red circle

from your husband—black circle

out of your own mouth in the last week—white circle

all of the above—blue circle

Come up with a few other statements on your own, based
on the ages and characteristics of your group.

Dig Deep

1. Which fears are worth having? Which fears are worth
   conquering? Have the women share opinions and
   examples of good fears and foolish fears. Are they different for each woman, or are there similarities?

2. Discuss the notion of anxiety being inherited. Does
   everyone agree that nervous parents have nervous
   children? Why do some people disagree with that statement? Where is it an explanation, and where is it an
   excuse? How would each of the women rate their own
   parent-child anxiety dynamic?

3. Have the women share experiences in which they have filtered well as parents and times when they failed to filter information for their children. These episodes may be similar to the ones discussed in question 1. How do they adapt their filter for each child, or do they adapt at all? What role could prayer play in gaining that filter in fearful situations?

Apply

1. Come up with two or three fearful parenting scenarios, such as diagnosis of a serious illness, injury to a child, death of a loved one, or Dad losing his job. Now apply the filtering process as a group. Divide a sheet of paper into two halves. On one side write all the thoughts likely to go through a mother's mind in that situation. Then, on the other side, come up with appropriately filtered ways to communicate those thoughts with children. Examine even further by discussing how that filter would be altered for different age groups.

2. Have the women make a list of their "foolish fears," such as speaking in public, heights, spiders, airplane travel, etc. Share a few of your own at first to help the women open up. Remind them that every fear, no matter how silly, feels real. Let each woman identify two steps she could take to overcome those fears. Brainstorm

ways each woman could be helped by a spouse, her children, or the group. Ask each woman to commit to accomplishing one of those steps between now and the end of the study.

3. If the women have a working knowledge of the Bible, make a list of biblical characters and their fears. Which ones faced those fears? What was the result for both them and the people around them? A few examples might be Esther, Daniel, Jacob's fear of Esau's retribution, Adam, and Peter walking on the water.

Pray

Thank God for the people who show us courage in our lives. Praise him for the unique blending of our families, for the compassion and love we can show our children and our children can show us.

Ask God's guidance in dealing with fears as a family. Invite the Holy Spirit to remind you to pray for guidance in difficult situations and to give you clear thoughts in crises. Praise God as the perfect author of our lives, able to work any situation for good if we let him.

Pray for God's protection over your children, that they will be shielded from information, images, and situations that are unhealthy. Pray for those children who are away from home at college, in military service, or in custody situations in which their parents cannot be near them. Ask God to provide long-distance blessings and guidance.

Chapter 9: The View

Icebreaker

Find the highest place in your church (or wherever you meet), such as the steeple, bell tower, choir loft, upper floor window, etc. Look out: What do you see? What can't you see from the ground? Now look down: What's dangerous? What's protecting you from that danger? Take a moment to explore a physical example of view's double-sided nature.

Dig Deep

1. Ask the women to share a moment when their instincts have told them to "look down." What told them a crucial moment was in the works? Is it something they perceived or an internal instinct? What were they doing at the time? Was it difficult to stop what they were doing? Make sure the discussion includes what the impact of that moment was for both them and their children.

2. How hard is it for each woman in your group to "welcome the worry"? Discuss Allie's statement that concern over parenting is the sign of an involved parent. Do the women agree or disagree? Are there situations

when that concept does not apply? Can the worry go too far or not far enough? It is often helpful to try to cite examples—but you must work to ensure the conversation does not fall into judgmental gossip.

3. How do hormones affect each woman in the group? Is it a mighty force or a minor annoyance? What about sleep? What other forces can work to skew a mother's viewpoint? Share what makes each of you crazy. You may find the commonalties surprisingly comforting.

Apply

1. Have someone suggest an example from their own life similar to CJ's toy or Mandy's "I hate you!" incident. Play "Get Inside Mom's Brain" and come up with all the statements that would go through a mother's internal dialogue when she faces that situation. Don't edit them for rationality, logic, or wisdom—make this a time of emotional brainstorming. When you've finished the list, identify which statements are valuable and which hinder—remember there will be valuable statements on both sides of the dialogue. Does the group agree on a course of action, or is the decision split?

2. Have each woman list eight things she does well as a parent. Now let each woman list two things she admires about the parenting of each mother in the group. When you are done, each woman will have a list of ten mothering attributes. If you'd like, compile the lists for each mother and put them in an inexpensive frame as a gift for your last meeting. Every mom needs a daily dose of affirmation.

3. Put the statement, "Every vice is a virtue gone three steps too far," to the test. List some challenging personality traits in children (such as persistence) that would become admirable qualities in adults. Where do the short-term frustrations in parenting bring long-term gains?

Pray

Pray for women in need of professional help. Ask God to send them resources and encouragement. Somewhere, at this very moment, a mother (or child) is at the very end of her rope and feeling hopeless. Pray for that person's courage to seek help. Ask God to grant us the sensitivity to help someone in our lives get the help she (or he) needs.

Pray for mental health professionals, that they may have wisdom, compassion, and strength to serve. Pray for your pastors as well, for they often serve in this way. If your community has a help line or crisis center, pray for its continued service, for its workers, and for the people who call upon its assistance.

Read Isaiah 41:10 aloud. Thank God for his promise to guide us. Let each woman lift up—silently or aloud—a situation in which she needs to feel God's hand upholding her. Read Isaiah 41:17–20 as a final blessing when you are done.

Chapter 10: The Finale

Icebreaker
Have each woman think of one fear she has either conquered or begun to face during the course of this study. Let each woman stand and name that fear and her progress toward not letting it master her, and applaud her. Make as much noise as you can, clapping and cheering. Encourage her to take a bow. Let anyone around you join in the applause (go around the building and gather an audience if you have to). If you've got a crafty gal in your group, have her make up a "Badge of Courage" to award to each mom as she takes her bow.

Dig Deep
1. Allie preferred the cards safely in The Box. Ask each woman what they would hide in a box if they could. What parenting challenge feels as though it's staring them down and they'd like it to go away? Why box it up? Why take it out and look at it?

2. Where does each woman feel alone in her parenting? Are there fears she is convinced no other mother faces? Has she proven that idea wrong—and that she is not alone—in any part of this study? What use has that realization been to her?

3. Like Allie's courage, most women have a virtue they're not sure how they acquired. What unearned-but-God-gifted strength does each woman feel she has? Does the fact that she can't explain how or why she got it cause her to doubt its validity? Let the women help each other identify strengths if they are having trouble identifying their own. What does it mean to accept such a gift from God?

Apply

1. Allie states, "Courage is a choice." Where in her life does each woman see that choice before her? Let each woman identify the place in her life right now in which she can make the choice of courage. What will that choice look like? What actions will be involved? Are there opportunities for encouragement and accountability within the group?

2. Give each of the women time to think about why God has placed each of her children in her care. What gifts can she give them? What gifts can they give her? Can she come to understand God's unique pairing of her and her children? Let other women in the group share their insights—sometimes others can see the gifts we bring our children more clearly than we can see them ourselves.

3. Have the women make a list of ten realizations this study has brought them. You can suggest they identify one for each chapter or just think of ten. List them down the left side of a sheet of paper. On the right side, opposite each realization, let the women think of a concrete action they can take based on that realization. Encourage them to place these goals somewhere where they will see them often.

Pray
Take some time to thank God for the work he has done in each woman throughout this study. Thank him for the relationships that have come about, for the insights that might engender new attitudes, and for the perfect pairing of each mother with her children.

Pray over the realizations and actions. Ask God to honor these efforts and to bless them with good fruit. Ask him boldly to send encouragement and commitment into each woman. Take him up on his promise of courage. If you are so inclined, the hymn "A Mighty Fortress Is Our God" speaks to this journey very well.

Pray for each child in each family. Ask God to protect them, to give them courage, and to help them one day know (if they don't already) how much God loves them and has marvelous plans for them. Praise God for the time you've spent together and the new blessings God has planned for each family. Ask him to keep each woman in the hearts of those in the group and to ensure the blessings of this study flow long after you have stopped meeting.

Dear Reader:

No one should have to go into the dark places alone. The call to companionship in this book extends from me to you as well. I would love to hear how this book affected you, what touched you, what bothered you, or what helped you.

If your mothers' group elected to read this book together, I'd be more than happy to visit you and hear your thoughts. If I can't come in person, find your way to a speakerphone and I'll visit you electronically. In any event, letters and e-mails are always, always welcome.

Of course, I always love the opportunity to come and speak to groups large and small.

Here are the ways you can get in touch with me:

Allie Pleiter
P.O. Box 7026
Villa Park, IL 60181
Website: www.alliepleiter.com
Email: alliepleiter@aol.com

Hearts at Home.

The Hearts at Home organization is committed to meeting the needs of women in the profession of motherhood. Founded in 1993, Hearts at Home offers a variety of resources and events to assist women in their jobs as wives and mothers.

Find out how Hearts at Home can provide you with ongoing education and encouragement in the profession of motherhood. In addition to this book, our resources include the *Hearts at Home* magazine, the *Hearts at Home* devotional, and our Hearts at Home website. Additionally, Hearts at Home events make a great getaway for individuals, moms' groups, or for that special friend, sister, or sister-in-law. The regional conferences, attended by over ten thousand women each year, provide a unique, affordable, and highly encouraging weekend for the woman who takes the profession of motherhood seriously.

Hearts at Home
900 W. College Ave.
Normal, Illinois 61761
Phone: (309) 888-MOMS
Fax (309) 888-4525
Email: hearts@hearts-at-home.org
Website: www.hearts-at-home.org

WOULD YOU LIKE ADDITIONAL RESOURCES FOR YOUR GROUP?

We hope your moms' group enjoyed this study. If you would like to enhance this learning opportunity by providing your group additional mothering resources, make a copy of the form below, fill in the information on the copy, and mail or fax it to Hearts at Home. Your resources are free of charge and will arrive within 3–6 weeks. (The form is also available on our website.)

Additionally, Hearts at Home maintains a comprehensive database of moms' groups in the United States. This allows us to operate as a clearinghouse for information about the groups. For instance, if a woman moves to a new community, she can contact Hearts at Home to locate a group in her area. If you would like to be part of the Moms Group Referral Network, please indicate below as well.

❏ Yes! Please send me resources for my group!

Please ship to:

Name of group: _____

Name of leader: _____

Shipping address: _____

_____

Contact name and phone number: _____

_____

Contact email:_____

How many women attend your group each week? _____

Please indicate all the resources you would like your group to receive:

❑ Conference Information Brochures (if available)
❑ *Hearts at Home* Magazine
❑ *Hearts at Home* Devotional

Other resources for moms' group leaders:

❑ Hearts at Home Video Order Form
❑ Hearts at Home Audio Tape Order Form

❑ Yes! Please include our group in your referral network!

Name of group _____

Meeting address _____

_____

Contact name and phone number _____

_____

Group website (if applicable) _____

Hearts at Home
900 W. College Ave.
Normal, Illinois 61761
Phone: (309) 888-MOMS
Fax (309) 888-4525
Email: hearts@hearts-at-home.org
Website: www.hearts-at-home.org

Professionalizing Motherhood

Encouraging, Educating, and Equipping Mothers at Home

Jill Savage, Founder and Director of Hearts at Home®

"Just a mom?" There's no such thing. Motherhood isn't a second-rate occupation. It is a career that can maximize your talents and strengths to their fullest. Look past the surface of mothering—the endless tasks and frantic pace—to the incredible skills required to raise your children and nurture your marriage. The truth is clear: You're a professional in one of the most dignified, demanding, and rewarding fields any woman can find.

Upbeat, candid, and engaging, *Professionalizing Motherhood* will do more than help you radically redefine how you see yourself. It will guide you toward practical development as a career woman who specializes in the home. Jill Savage helps you determine a strategy and set goals for professional training and growth. From the foundational to the practical, you'll learn about

- Establishing the mission of your job
- Developing a network of "coworkers"
- The all-important foundation of knowing your value in Christ
- How marriage and mothering work together
- Organizational and homemaking basics
- Taking care of your personal needs
- And much more

Professionalizing Motherhood casts a fresh and meaningful vision for mothering as a worthy career choice for this season of your life. Get ready to be inspired as you discover how profoundly meaningful and influential a profession motherhood is.

Softcover: 0-310-24817-5

Is There Really Sex After Kids?

A Mom-to-Mom Chat on the Realities of Keeping Intimacy Alive After Kids

Jill Savage, Founder and Director of Hearts at Home®

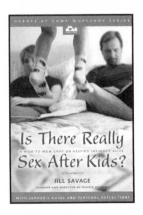

"What's happened to our sex life now that we have kids?" Many moms may not ask the question aloud, but Jill Savage knows from her years of leading Hearts at Home conferences that no workshop subject will more quickly fill a room.

Having children at home does alter the sexual dynamic between husband and wife. Going from making meatloaf to making love, from practical mommy to passionate lover, all in the course of one crowded evening has its own set of unique challenges.

Written by a mom, for moms, and filled with practical ideas that have helped moms *Is There Really Sex After Kids* is not a clinical book on sexual technique, though readers will find some creative suggestions. It isn't a counselor's text, though readers will find the sage wisdom of a mentor and friend. It is a woman-to-woman discussion, a true insider's look, at what works to build intimacy outside the bedroom and improve intimacy inside the bedroom.

Wonderfully practical, written with empathy and humor, *Is There Really Sex After Kids* is designed to help women rise above the frustrations and disappointments of what has happened to their sex lives now that they have kids in the house, and to help them restore intimacy, pleasure, spontaneity, and passion in their marriages.

Softcover: 0-310-23743-2

Pick up a copy today at your favorite bookstore!

ZONDERVAN™

GRAND RAPIDS, MICHIGAN 49530 USA

WWW.ZONDERVAN.COM

Creating the Moms Group You've Been Looking For

Your How-To Manual for Connecting with Other Moms

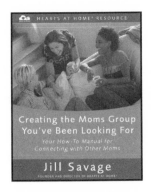

Jill Savage, Founder and Director of Hearts at Home®

Drawing from her experience as founder of Hearts at Home®, author Jill Savage shows women how moms groups will help keep their vision fresh, improve their skills, and enable them to experience a sense of accomplishment in the profession of motherhood.

People who are involved in professional development activities are enriched by a sense of "belonging" and stay in their profession longer. Women in the profession of motherhood need professional affiliations as well!

Creating the Moms Group You've Been Looking For is a valuable resource manual providing moms with everything they need to know to start and improve effective mom's ministries. The book supplies women with the vision and the know how to start a moms group. It is also a consultation manual for women already in a group who want to take their group or their leadership to the next level. This manual provides church leaders with a comprehensive view of a mothers ministry

Softcover: 0-310-25447-7

Pick up a copy today at your favorite bookstore!